KNOWING THE FATHER

Colin Dye

Sovereign World

Sovereign World Ltd
PO Box 777
Tonbridge
Kent TN11 0ZS
England

Scriptural quotations are from the New King James Version, Thomas Nelson Inc., 1991.

ISBN 1 85240 206 7

This Sovereign World book is distributed in North America by Renew Books, a ministry of Gospel Light, Ventura, California, USA. For a free catalog of resources from Renew Books/Gospel Light, please contact your Christian supplier or call 1-800-4-GOSPEL.

Typeset by CRB Associates, Reepham, Norfolk
Printed in England by Clays Ltd, St Ives plc.

FOREWORD

The material in this *Sword of the Spirit* series has been developed over the past ten years at Kensington Temple in London as we have sought to train leaders for the hundreds of churches and groups we have established. Much of the material was initially prepared for the students who attend the International Bible Institute of London – which is based at our church.

Over the years, other churches and colleges have asked if they may use some of our material to help them establish training courses for leaders in their towns and countries. This series has been put together partly to meet this growing need, as churches everywhere seek to train large numbers of new leaders to serve the growth that God is giving.

The material has been constantly refined – by myself, by the students as they have responded, by my many associate pastors, and by the staff at the Bible Institute. In particular, my colleague Timothy Pain has been responsible for sharpening, developing and shaping my different courses and notes into this coherent series.

I hope that many people will use this series in association with our developing Satellite Bible School, but I also pray that churches around the world will use the books to train leaders.

We live at a time when increasing numbers of new churches are being started, and I am sure that we will see even more startling growth in the next few decades. It is vital that we re-examine the way we train and release leaders so that these new churches have the best possible biblical foundation. This series is our contribution to equipping tomorrow's leaders with the eternal truths that they need.

Colin Dye

CONTENTS

INTRODUCTION

I doubt whether there are many Christians who do not know that God is three persons – the Father, the Son and the Spirit. They may not all appreciate the significance of God's triune nature, they may not all understand the full biblical basis for the Trinity, but the vast majority have been taught that their living God is somehow 'Three-in-One'.

I also suspect that every believer throughout the world can describe the Second Person of God – the Son – in some detail. They know what he is like and what he has done for them: they can speak about him with some accuracy to any uncommitted person.

Furthermore, in the last thirty years, there has been a widespread re-awakening to the Third Person of God. In every Christian tradition, believers have begun increasingly to appreciate and to experience the distinctive Person and ministry of the Holy Spirit. Again, many might struggle to describe him, but most know what he does.

Yet it is all rather different when we consider the First Person of God. Most believers today appear to confuse the triune God with the First Person of God. They know that God is the Father, but they find it difficult to distinguish between the general fatherhood of Almighty God and the specific nature and ministry of God the Father.

It has been said that Evangelicalism is a Jesus movement, that Pentecostalism is a Spirit movement, and that the Orthodox tradition is a Father movement. But this should not be so, for *every* branch of the church is meant to be filled with Father-focused believers.

Everything that the Son has done, and still does, is so that we can know the Father. Everything that the Spirit does is to enable us to live in the Father's presence and to fellowship intimately with him. Sadly, if we do not know the Father – and do not know what it means to be children of the Father in his world – the Son has died in vain.

This is a book for believers who are willing to set aside their own ideas about God, and to study God's Word to discover God's revelation about himself. We need to find out what the Scriptures teach about the general fatherhood of God, and – especially – what they reveal about the First Person of God, about the Father.

Please make sure that you read each scriptural reference – and tick the margin reference boxes as you go along to show that you have. Answer every question and think through each point as it is made. Before moving on to a new section, think carefully about the implications of what you have studied. Please allow God to speak to you about your relationship with the Father as you study his word.

At the end of the book, there is some activity material and questions. Please make sure that you study Parts 1–9 before beginning to work through the activities, as this will ensure that you have an overview of the biblical teaching about the Father before you try to apply the details of any one area. These questions will help you to grasp and apply the scriptural material that you have studied.

You will also be able to use the activity pages when you teach the material to small groups. Please feel free to photocopy these pages and distribute them to any group you are leading. Although you should work through all the questions when you are studying on your own, please don't expect a small group to cover all the material. Instead, prayerfully select those parts that you think are most relevant for your group. This means that, at some meetings you might use all the material whilst at others you might use only a small part.

By the time you finish this book, it is my prayer that you will have a better understanding of the name and nature of the triune God, that you will have begun to know the First Person of God much more deeply, and that you will have started to revel in the wonderful freedom of the sons and daughters of 'Abba', our gracious heavenly Father.

Colin Dye

PART ONE

who is god?

The Bible never tries to prove that God exists; it simply asserts the fact of his existence as a self-evident reality. From Genesis 1:1 to Revelation 22:18–19, the Bible expounds the truth that God exists. Yet it always explains *who* he is, not *why* or *how* he is.

In passages like Psalm 14:1, the Bible acknowledges that there are people who deny God's existence. But it dismisses their belief as 'foolishness'. As far as the Bible is concerned, the truth about God is so obvious that only a fool would ever reject it.

This 'foolishness' has become the basis of much modern thinking, and is a distinguishing mark of our age. We must recognise, however, that contemporary beliefs like 'atheism' and 'humanism' are essentially spiritual ideas, and not intellectual constructions.

Proving God

God cannot be proved or disproved by philosophical argument or scientific enquiry: he can be known only through a spiritual revelation which is received by faith. But our living faith must never be mindless.

Genesis 1:1 ☐

Revelation
     22:18–19 ☐

Psalm 14:1 ☐

Throughout the centuries, Christian thinkers have proposed four main philosophical arguments for God's existence. These do not 'prove' that God exists; they merely show that our belief in him is logical and reasonable.

1.   the cosmological argument

This states that the very existence of the world, the *cosmos*, points to a 'first cause', or to a creator, who brought it into being.

2.   the teleological argument

This suggests that the presence of *telos*, of design and purpose, in the universe points to a creator or architect who designed it.

3.   the moral argument

This maintains that the human sense of morality indicates a moral governor of the universe who holds us responsible for our actions.

4.   the ontological argument

This argues that the widespread human concept of God itself implies that he actually exists.

Although no intellectual argument can ever be conclusive, these four ideas do have considerable value – particularly when they are deeply grasped and developed. Their primary importance for believers, however, is their demonstration that belief in God is consistent with good logic and reason rather than muddled and mindless.

Knowing God

The Bible consistently explains *who* God is by revealing his nature and character. It is vital, however, that we understand *how* this revelation is made.

The Bible does not define God; instead, it introduces him. It reveals him personally, rather than propositionally. Instead of offering abstract facts about God, it presents him in the context of relationships with ordinary people.

We must remember that God's great desire is for people to know him, not just to know about him. Although, in this book, we are seeking to understand the biblical teaching about who God is and what he is like, our seeking must be set in the context of our personal relationship with him. Our aim in learning about God from the Scriptures must be to love him more deeply, to follow him even more closely and to know him ever more intimately.

We see this idea of 'revelation by relationship' in, for example, Psalm 139. We could say this Psalm suggests that:

Psalm 139 ☐

- *God is omniscient* – verses 1–6 show that he is all-knowing

- *God is omnipresent* – verses 7–12 teach that he is everywhere

- *God is omnipotent* – verses 13–16 demonstrate his power and skill

- *God is holy* – verses 17–24 point to his purity and holiness

But technical words like 'omniscience' and 'omnipotence' are too dry and too abstract to communicate the true meaning of Psalm 139.

The Psalmist is not trying to define God propositionally by presenting him as all-knowing; he is celebrating the fact that his God knows everything about him. And he is not trying to establish the principle of God's omnipresence; he is rejoicing in the truth that his God is with him wherever he is.

The revelation about God in Psalm 139 is personal, practical, relational and immediate. The Psalmist does not just know truths about God, he also knows his God deeply and intimately.

As we consider the scriptural teaching about God, and – especially – about the first person of the Trinity, we must keep on reminding ourselves that we are not examining abstract truths about a theoretical deity. Instead, we are grasping the means by which we can deepen a living, personal relationship with our very own heavenly Father.

THE BEING AND ATTRIBUTES OF GOD

The Bible contains a wealth of teaching about God's nature and characteristics, and the rest of the material in this chapter merely offers a very basic overview of the scriptural teaching. For the sake of clarity, the material has been divided into distinct categories; but God is all of these things, all of the time. Each aspect of his nature is inter-related with all other aspects, and is equally important. Error creeps in when any aspect of God's being is over-emphasised or overlooked.

God is eternal

God's 'eternity' is the most basic biblical idea about God – and a right understanding of God hinges on appreciating the consequences of his eternal nature.

Two aspects of God's being are wrapped together in the one English word 'eternal'.

1. The eternity of God means that he had no beginning and will have no end. He himself is the source of time and matter, of life and existence. Although God does give his children the gift of eternal life, our eternity differs from his in that ours has a beginning.

    We see this 'beyond time' aspect of God's eternal nature in passages like Genesis 21:33; Deuteronomy 33:27; Psalm 48:14; 90:1–2; Isaiah 40:28 & 57:15.

2. The eternity of God also means that he is unchanging, as change is something which is comprehensible and possible only within time. 'Unceasing' and 'unchanging' are, therefore, the two equal and inseparable meanings of the one word 'eternity'. We see the unchanging aspect of God's eternal nature in, for example, Numbers 23:9; 1 Samuel 15:29; Malachi 3:6 and James 1:17.

God is infinite

The eternity of God also implies his infinity. Technically, God's eternity shows that he is not bound by the limitations of time, whereas his infinity shows that he is not bound by the limitations of space.

Christians, however, use 'eternal' as a shorthand way of showing that God is beyond *everything* because he is the source of everything.

By definition, every aspect of God's nature – his love, power, provision, knowledge, salvation, and so on – must exist 'eternally and infinitely'. Because God is unceasing and unchanging, there must be an 'eternal-and-infinite' capacity and quality to everything that he is, everything that he has and everything that he does.

Genesis 21:33 ☐

Deuteronomy 33:27 ☐

Psalm 48:14 ☐
90:1–2 ☐

Isaiah 40:28 ☐
57:15 ☐

Numbers 23:9 ☐

1 Samuel 15:29 ☐

Malachi 3:6 ☐

James 1:17 ☐

This is hard to grasp because we are ourselves bound by time and space. It is important, however, that we remember God's eternity whenever we consider any aspect of his nature.

Every facet of the Father that we study in this book is, by definition, infinite, eternal, unceasing and unchanging. This foundation fact should inspire us to greater faith and deeper worship.

God is immortal

God is not only 'beyond' time and space because he created time and space; he is also beyond life – because he created life itself and every form of life. Many of the words that we use to describe God involve images of time, space and life. Although some of these appear to deny his eternal nature, they help us to comprehend his divine nature.

1 Timothy 1:17 ☐

John 5:26 ☐

We say 'God exists forever' because this is a simple way of grasping his eternal nature. And we describe him as 'a great or high God' because it helps us appreciate his infinite nature. The full truth, however, is that God is before-and-beyond time, space, matter and life. He cannot be bound or defined by any of these things, because he existed before them and brought them into being.

We also say 'God lives', and we call him 'the living God', because these metaphors help us to celebrate his vital, vibrant being. Yet these expressions are merely feeble, human attempts to help us grasp the majestic wonder of his divine immortality.

When we say that God is immortal, we do not simply mean that God will not die, or even that he cannot die. God's immortality actually means that he is 'not mortal', that he is 'before-and-beyond life'.

Believers who describe God's existence in terms of 'living forever' need to recognise that they are using a limited physical picture. It is probably more accurate for us to think in terms of God being 'the source of all life' rather than as being merely 'alive'. God will not die because he existed eternally before he created life. His immortality means that he is much, much more than 'living forever'.

The full truth is that God is not sourced in anything or sustained by anything. He is himself the source of space, life and time, and he is the eternal sustainer of these things. He is entirely self-sufficient and owes his existence to nothing outside himself. Quite simply, he is 'immortal'.

God is transcendent

Several English words are used to describe the biblical idea that God's eternal nature means he is far beyond everything in the universe.

For example, God is described as 'transcendent'. This means that he exists apart from the material universe and is not subject to its inherent limitations. It is derived from the Latin verb *transcendere*, which means 'to climb over', and is used to convey the idea that God is far beyond our reach, that he is much higher than we are.

God is also described as 'exalted'. This word comes from the Latin word *altare*, which means 'high'. It also means that God is raised high, that he is far above us, far above the universe.

In the Bible, God is commonly named as *El Elyon*, 'the Most High'; and this points to his supreme transcendence and exaltation. We see this, for example, in Genesis 14:18–22; Numbers 24:16; Deuteronomy 32:8; 1 Samuel 2:10; 2 Samuel 22:14; Psalm 7:17; 21:7; 50:14; 78:17; 83:18; 92:1; 107:11; Isaiah 14:14.

The Bible often encourages us to worship God because he is infinitely higher, or exalted, above everything. We see this in Nehemiah 9:5; Psalm 47:2; 92:8 & 97:9.

Isaiah 57:15 also points to God's lofty status, but it shows that God's transcendence must not be over-emphasised. Because God is infinite, he is not only *above* all things, he is also *alongside* all things.

God is spirit

John 4:24 summarises God's exalted, eternal, infinite, immortal nature in one short word: he is spirit. This means that he is not directly accessible to our human physical senses. We see this, for example, in John 1:18; 1 Timothy 1:17 & 6:15–16.

Because God is essentially spiritual, he cannot be physically seen, touched, heard, tasted or smelt. Of course, most Christians do talk about 'hearing' God and 'touching' him. When we do this, however, we are using physical words metaphorically to describe our spiritual 'faith-sensing'.

As God is spirit, we cannot not see him with our eyes or hear him with our ears; instead we know him in our *spirits* by our *faith*.

Genesis
    14:18–22 ☐

Numbers 24:16 ☐

Deuteronomy
    32:8 ☐

1 Samuel 2:10 ☐

2 Samuel 22:14 ☐

Psalm 7:17 ☐
    21:7 ☐
    50:14 ☐
    78:17 ☐
    83:18 ☐
    92:1 ☐
    107:11 ☐

Isaiah 14:14 ☐

Nehemiah 9:5 ☐

Psalm 47:2 ☐
    92:8 ☐
    97:9 ☐

Isaiah 57:15 ☐

John 4:24 ☐
    1:18 ☐

1 Timothy 1:17 ☐
    6:15–16 ☐

It is helpful to keep on reminding people that God is spirit – and to make it plain, therefore, that he is experienced spiritually. Physical words like 'hear' and 'see' are useful, but only to those who appreciate that they are metaphors and not literally applicable.

God is the only God

The Bible shows that there is only one God: there is none besides him. When we grasp God's exaltation, eternity and immortality, it is obvious that there cannot be another god. There simply can be only *one* supreme, eternal and infinite being – a second such being is impossible.

Of course, the Scriptures recognise that people often invent gods and offer them worship; but these are not genuine divine beings. He is *'the'* God of heaven and earth.

We see this truth in passages like Genesis 24:3, 7; Exodus 18:11; Deuteronomy 4:34–35; 6:4; 7:9; 10:17; Joshua 2:11; 2 Chronicles 2:5–6; Ezra 5:11–12; 6:9–10; 7:12, 23; Nehemiah 1:4–5; 2:4, 20; Isaiah 54:5; Jeremiah 10:10–11 and Daniel 2:47.

God is immanent

We have noted that too great an emphasis on any one aspect of God's nature inevitably leads people into error. God's transcendence, or exaltation, is, perhaps, the aspect of his being which has been most frequently over-emphasised.

God's *transcendence* does mean that he is 'up there' and 'out there'. But this must be balanced by an equal emphasis on his *immanence*.

The English word 'immanent' comes from the Latin word *manere*, which means 'to remain' or 'to dwell'. When we describe God as 'immanent', we are asserting that he permanently pervades the universe – that he dwells here, that he remains and does not leave. We can think of Psalm 139 as a magnificent celebration of God's 'immanence'.

If God is eternal-and-infinite, he must, by definition, be everywhere. He must be *both* transcendent *and* immanent. If we emphasise just one of these aspects of his character, we are implicitly denying the other.

Christians often use a metaphor which celebrates God's transcendence: they say that he 'holds the whole world in his hands'.

Genesis 24:3, 7 ☐

Exodus 18:11 ☐

Deuteronomy
  4:34–35 ☐
  6:4 ☐
  7:9 ☐
  10:17 ☐

Joshua 2:11 ☐

2 Chronicles
  2:5–6 ☐

Ezra 5:11–12 ☐
  6:9–10 ☐
  7:12, 23 ☐

Nehemiah 1:4–5 ☐
  2:4, 20 ☐

Isaiah 54:5 ☐

Jeremiah
  10:10–11 ☐

Daniel 2:47 ☐

Psalm 139 ☐

But the world is not just surrounded by God, it is also permeated by him. As we see throughout this book, God's eternal, infinite, immortal, spiritual nature must, by definition, be packed with paradoxes.

While it is true to say that he holds the world in his hands, we should also say – like Jeremiah 23:23–24 – the balancing truth that he fills the whole world with his presence.

Because God is infinite, he must, by definition, be everywhere. He is both exalted *and* Emmanuel – the 'Most High' *and* 'God with us'. We must not imagine this truth, however, in terms of God being spread very thinly: this is completely wrong. The infinite nature of God must mean that all of him is everywhere. Nothing else makes sense.

God is as much here as he is there. He is fully with me, and he is fully with all other believers too. This is what it means to be eternal, infinite, immanent and omnipresent.

God is personal

Most of God's attributes are obvious consequences of his eternity. The Bible, however, also presents God as a person – never as an 'it', a 'thing', a 'principle', a 'power' or a 'force'. It clearly reveals that God has all the attributes of personality. For example:

- *He thinks* – Isaiah 40:13–14

- *He wills* – Ephesians 1:11

- *He feels love* – Hosea 11:1

- *He feels anger* – Numbers 25:3

- *He feels compassion* – Psalm 103:13

- *He feels joy* – Zephaniah 3:17

Genesis 1:27 states that God has created personal beings – men and women – *in his image*: this implies that God himself must also be a personal being. The Bible reinforces this by always using personal pronouns for God – 'I', 'my', 'his', 'he', and so on. And, as we will see in Part Two, it repeatedly gives God personal names.

As we work through the biblical revelation of God, we need to maintain a strong grip on the paradox of God's eternal-and-personal nature. If we over-stress his eternity, we will not believe that we can

Jeremiah 23:23–24 ☐

Isaiah 40:13–14 ☐

Ephesians 1:11 ☐

Hosea 11:1 ☐

Numbers 25:3 ☐

Psalm 103:13 ☐

Zephaniah 3:17 ☐

Genesis 1:27 ☐

know him. And if we over-emphasise God's personhood, we will doubt his magnificent infinite greatness. Instead, we need to hold these two divine characteristics in their scriptural creative tension.

God is triune

As we will see in Part Four, the New Testament teaches that God is one eternal being whose essence exists in three persons. The Father, the Son and the Spirit, however, are not three distinct individuals; they are three self-distinctions within one being.

God is one, he is not divided into three. But he reveals himself to men and women in a threefold diversity of persons, characteristics and functions whom we know as Father, Son and Spirit.

We see this, for example, in Matthew 28:19; Mark 1:9–11; John 14:16–17, 25–26; 15:26; 16:13–15; Romans 8; 1 Corinthians 12:3–6; 2 Corinthians 13:14; Galatians 4:4–6; Ephesians 4:4–6; 2 Thessalonians 2:13–14; Titus 3:4–6; 1 Peter 1:2; Jude 1:20–21 and Revelation 1:4.

In this *Sword of the Spirit* series, we consider each divine person in a different book, in *Knowing the Father*, *Knowing the Spirit* and *Knowing the Son*. Nevertheless, we must always remember that the three divine persons are each fully God, and that they together form the one spiritual being whom we call God. We consider the triune nature of God more fully in Parts Four and Five.

God is creator

The Bible reveals that God spoke our great universe into existence. As God is eternal-and-infinite, creation cannot be the limit of his power: Job 26:14 shows that it is merely a tiny glimpse into his infinite omnipotence.

Many modern believers make little of God's creative nature: they have been silenced by the opponents of God. But God's essential creativity is one of the most emphasised scriptural themes.

We see this, for example, in Genesis 1:1; Job 4:17; 35:10; 36:3; 38:1–39:30; Psalm 8:3; 95:6; 115:15; 119:73; 121:2; 124:8; 146:6; Isaiah 27:11; Jeremiah 10:16; Hosea 8:14; John 5:26; Romans 11:35–36; Hebrews 11:3; Revelation 3:14 & 4:11.

Matthew 28:19 ☐
Mark 1:9–11 ☐
John 14:16–17 ☐
14:25–26 ☐
15:26 ☐
16:13–15 ☐
1 Corinthians 12:3–6 ☐
2 Corinthians 13:14 ☐
Galatians 4:4–6 ☐
Ephesians 4:4–6 ☐
2 Thessalonians 2:13–14 ☐
Titus 3:4–6 ☐
1 Peter 1:2 ☐
Jude 1:20–21 ☐
Revelation 1:4 ☐
Job 26:14 ☐
Genesis 1:1 ☐
Job 4:17 ☐
35:10 ☐
38–39 ☐
Psalm 8:3 ☐
95:6 ☐
119:73 ☐
121:2 ☐
146:6 ☐
Isaiah 27:11 ☐
Jeremiah 10:16 ☐
Hosea 8:14 ☐
John 5:26 ☐
Romans 11:35–36 ☐
Hebrews 11:3 ☐
Revelation 3:14 ☐
4:11 ☐

The Bible does not teach *how* God creates; it merely ascribes creation to his wisdom and power. No matter how far the boundaries of human science extend, nobody can ever discover how matter, space and time came into being out of nothing.

People must hold one of only three possible beliefs – there are no other alternatives.

1. *Matter and energy have always existed; they are the ultimate reality: life and the time-space universe are the results of their totally random activity.*

2. *Matter and energy spontaneously came into being out of nothing, without – by definition – any cause or explanation.*

3. *A wholly-other, wholly-beyond, wholly non-material being created space, time, matter, energy and life.*

Our choice between these three beliefs is entirely a spiritual decision, and not at all a scientific or intellectual decision. People need an equal amount of 'faith' whichever explanation they choose to follow.

God is sustainer

The Scriptures show that God did not leave our world devoid of his caring, creative presence. He continually watches over it and sustains it by his love and power. We see this, for example, in Nehemiah 9:6; Psalm 104:10–23; Acts 14:15–17.

Nehemiah 9:6 ☐

Psalm 104:10–23 ☐

Acts 14:15–17 ☐

God's all-sustaining nature is an obvious consequence of his eternity and infinity. As God, by definition, is unceasing and unchanging, he cannot distance himself from his act of creation or cease to be involved creatively with creation.

If the 'burst of divine energy' which brought the universe into being was an expression of the eternal-and-infinite God, it could not have been a momentary, temporal flash. This means that the existence of creation is, in itself, the evidence of God's sustainment.

God is sovereign

The Bible also identifies God not just as creator and sustainer, but also as the sovereign of the universe.

We see this, for example, in 1 Chronicles 29:25; Psalm 7:8; 10:16; 22:28; 47:2–8; 74:12; 99:2; 95:3–5; 103:19; 115:3; 135:6; Isaiah 46:6–11; 54:5; Jeremiah 10:7; Ezekiel 20:33; Daniel 2:47; 4:25–26, 32–37; Zechariah 14:9 and Ephesians 1:11.

These passages show that God governs, or rules, all things by his supreme power. He controls everything, and is infinitely active in the world as he works out his eternal purpose.

God is holy

The Bible teaches that each self-expression of God is perfectly holy. We see this, for example, in:

- *the Father* – Luke 1:49; John 17:11; 1 Peter 1:15–16; Revelation 4:8; 6:10

- *the Son* – Luke 1:35; Acts 3:14; 4:27–30; 1 John 2:20

- *the Spirit* – 2 Timothy 1:14; Titus 3:5; 2 Peter 1:21; Jude 20

For many people, the word 'holy' has moral associations. They think that holiness means being good and well-behaved; but the Hebrew and Greek words for 'holy', *qadosh* and *hagios*, are functional words which primarily mean 'totally separated to a single purpose' and 'devoted or consecrated to a particular cause'.

The triune God is 'holy' in the sense that he is *separated* from all creation by his exalted, eternal, infinite, sinless, morally perfect and spiritual nature: he is 'wholly other', 'wholly beyond'.

This means that the 'holiness' of God is the consequence of the sum of his attributes, and it is this which sets him apart from everything else. We see this, for example, in Exodus 3:5; Leviticus 19:2; Isaiah 6:2–3; 57:15 & 1 John 1:5.

But the members of the Trinity – the Father, the Son and the Spirit – are also 'holy' in the sense that they are totally *devoted* or consecrated to each other.

For example, we can say that Jesus reveals his holiness in his absolute consecration to the Father; and that the Spirit reveals his holiness in the way he exists only to bring glory to Jesus. The absolute commitment of the three divine persons to each other is their holiness.

1 Chronicles
29:25 ☐
Psalm 7:8 ☐
10:16 ☐
22:28 ☐
47:2–8 ☐
74:12 ☐
99:2 ☐
95:3–5 ☐
103:19 ☐
115:3 ☐
135:6 ☐
Isaiah 46:6–11 ☐
54:5 ☐
Jeremiah 10:7 ☐
Ezekiel 20:33 ☐
Daniel 2:47 ☐
4:25–26 ☐
4:32–37 ☐
Zechariah 14:9 ☐
Ephesians 1:11 ☐
Luke 1:49 ☐
John 17:11 ☐
1 Peter 1:15–16 ☐
Revelation 4:8 ☐
6:10 ☐
Luke 1:35 ☐
Acts 3:14 ☐
4:27–30 ☐
1 John 2:20 ☐
2 Timothy 1:14 ☐
Titus 3:5 ☐
2 Peter 1:21 ☐
Jude 20 ☐
Exodus 3:5 ☐
Leviticus 19:2 ☐
Isaiah 6:2–3 ☐
57:15 ☐
1 John 1:5 ☐

God is omnipotent and omniscient

The Bible constantly reminds us that God is omnipotent, is all-powerful, is all-mighty. We see this, for example, in Genesis 18:14; Jeremiah 32:27–28 and Zechariah 8:6.

The Bible also points out that he is omniscient or all-knowing. Because God is infinite, his knowledge is unlimited, and is not derived from anyone or anything outside himself. We see this, for example, in 1 Samuel 2:3; Psalm 139:1–6; Hebrews 4:13 & Deuteronomy 29:29.

Some people struggle with the idea of God's omniscience, because they think that his 'foreknowledge' is a fundamental denial of humanity's free will. But the fact that God knows all things does not mean that he wills all things. His *permissive* will, his allowing, is often very different from his *perfect* will. We consider the Father's will in Part Seven.

Again, God's omnipotence and omniscience are obvious consequences of his eternal-and-infinite personal nature. Every aspect of his being exists infinitely, which means that he is all-everything, always.

God is love

Finally, the Bible makes it abundantly clear that the essence of God is love. In fact, it is more accurate to say that he is all-love, or all-loving.

We see this, for example, in Exodus 34:6–7; Nehemiah 9:17, 31; Psalm 59:10–17; 103:8; Lamentations 3:22–23; Joel 2:13; Jonah 4:2; Nahum 1:2–3 & 1 John 4:8.

Because God is, by definition, infinitely and eternally loving, it must follow that everything he is, does and says must be motivated by, and filled with, infinite 'unceasing and unchanging' love.

All that we have learnt in this chapter about the triune God is, of course, also fully true for the Father, and for the Son, and for the Spirit. In this book, however, we are focusing on *Knowing the Father*; therefore we are concentrating on understanding the implications and application of God's attributes for our relationship with our heavenly Father.

PART TWO

the name of god

The Bible records over three hundred different names of God, and these contain a rich revelation of his person and character – and of his purposes for humanity.

Names generally mean little to us today. We use them as mere 'labels' to identify one person from another. But it was not like this in biblical times.

WHAT'S IN A NAME?

Scriptural names are usually significant. It seems that some parents tried to express their children's characters in the names that they gave them. The parents of Nabal, which means 'fool', cannot have been pleased with their son – and nor was his wife in 1 Samuel 25:25!

1 Samuel 25:25 ☐

In later life, some people's names were replaced or altered to match their characters: in the Old Testament, for example, Abram, Sarai and

Jacob became Abraham, Sarah, and Israel. And, in the New Testament, Simon and Joseph were also called Peter and Barnabas.

Some biblical names reflect birth circumstances, as in Genesis 10:25; 19:22 & 25:30. Others are prophetic, as in Genesis 25:26. Most biblical names, however, indicate the faith of the parents rather than the character of the child.

But the names by which God chose to make himself known to his people are not coloured by any human weakness, circumstance or limitation. God's names are a vital part of the revelation by which he leads his people into the knowledge of himself.

'The name of God'

Although there are very many different names of God, with each one revealing a distinct aspect of his character and grace, the phrase 'the name of God' or 'the name of the Lord' is itself frequently used in the Old Testament.

'The name of the Lord' stands for God himself. It refers to the total revelation of all that is known about him. For example,

- *'the name of the Lord' was proclaimed to Moses when God passed before him and announced his nature* – Exodus 34:5–6

- *to 'call upon the name of the Lord' was to worship him as God* – Genesis 21:33; 26:25

- *to 'forget his name' was to depart from God* – Jeremiah 23:27

- *to 'take the name of the Lord in vain' was to affront his divine majesty* – Exodus 20:7

We can say that the phrase 'the name of God' encapsulates the full glorious nature and character of God. It points to the total manifestation of God to his people.

In the Old Testament, God's name was the pledge of all that he had promised to be to Israel and to do for them. We see this, for example, in 1 Samuel 12:22 and Psalm 25:11.

The phrase, 'the name of the Lord', enshrined the most important facts of Israel's revelation and experience of God. The all-powerful Maker of heaven and earth was their God. He had called them into a

Genesis 10:25 ☐
19:22 ☐
25:30 ☐
25:26 ☐

Exodus 34:5–6 ☐

Genesis 21:33 ☐
26:25 ☐

Jeremiah 23:27 ☐

Exodus 20:7 ☐

1 Samuel 12:22 ☐

Psalm 25:11 ☐

covenant relationship of grace. And the conviction that God would never deny his covenant, or go back on his promises, lies behind almost every use of the phrase, 'the name of the Lord'.

The name is the person

In the Bible, a name is never a tag; it is always the person. The new man, Abraham, is the new name, Abraham. The new man, Israel, is the new name, Israel, and so on.

This equation between 'name' and 'bearer of the name' can be seen, for example, in the idea that personal death is expressed by:

- *cutting off the name* – Joshua 7:9

- *destroying the name* – Deuteronomy 7:24

- *taking away the name* – Numbers 27:4

- *blotting out the name* – 2 Kings 14:27

- *rotting the name* – Proverbs 10:7

This association between name and person is seen most plainly in God, who is called repeatedly, 'the Name' – for example, Leviticus 24:11; Proverbs 18:10; Isaiah 30:27.

This is particularly clear in the New Testament, where:

- *Jesus promised to be where two or three gathered in the name* – Matthew 18:20

- *He taught his disciples to pray in the name* – John 14:13–14

- *He pledged that the Father would give in the name* – John 15:16; 16:23–24

- *He warned that his disciples would be hated because of the name* – Matthew 10:22

- *He guaranteed an abundant reward for whatever his disciples forsook for the sake of the name* – Matthew 19:29

- *Peter and John were forbidden to preach and teach in the name* – Acts 4:18; 5:28

- *Peter and John rejoiced that they were worthy to suffer for the name* – Acts 5:41

Joshua 7:9 ☐

Deuteronomy 7:24 ☐

Numbers 27:4 ☐

2 Kings 14:27 ☐

Proverbs 10:7 ☐

Leviticus 24:11 ☐

Proverbs 18:10 ☐

Isaiah 30:27 ☐

Matthew 18:20 ☐

John 14:13–14 ☐
15:16 ☐
16:23–24 ☐

Matthew 10:22 ☐
19:29 ☐

Acts 4:18 ☐
5:28 ☐
5:41 ☐

Acts 10:43 ☐
9:14, 21 ☐
16:18 ☐
19:17 ☐

Romans 10:13 ☐

Isaiah 30:27 ☐

Exodus 33:12 ☐
3:13 ☐
Psalm 22:22 ☐
John 17:6 ☐
Acts 9:15 ☐

Psalm 89:15–16 ☐
89:24 ☐
96:2 ☐
99:3 ☐
100:4–5 ☐
109:21 ☐
138:2 ☐
148:13 ☐

- *they preached forgiveness through the name* – Acts 10:43

- *the church comprised all who called on the name* – Acts 9:14, 21

- *Paul cast out a demon in the name* – Acts 16:18

- *through miracles, the name was glorified* – Acts 19:17

- *whoever calls on the name will be saved* – Romans 10:13

The name reveals the nature of God

When we read the Old Testament today, it is easy to wonder why passages like Isaiah 30:27 describe 'the name of the Lord coming', rather than 'God coming'.

We need to remember that 'the name' gathers together everything that is known about a person; and that, therefore, the use of 'the name' in the Bible refers to *the total revealed nature* of God. This means that 'the name' refers to God in the eternal fullness of his infinite power, holiness, grace, love, and so on.

We can see this idea in Exodus 33:12, when Moses expressed God's deep and intimate knowledge of him by saying that God 'knew him by name'. It is also apparent in Exodus 3:13, when Moses asked God for his name so that he could reveal God's nature to the people of Israel. A similar idea is present in Psalm 22:22; John 17:6 and Acts 9:15.

The Psalms link God's name with many different self-revelatory actions. They associate his name with, for example, his:

- *righteousness* – Psalm 89:15–16

- *faithfulness* – Psalm 89:24

- *salvation* – Psalm 96:2

- *holiness* – Psalm 99:3

- *goodness* – Psalm 100:4–5

- *mercy* – Psalm 109:21

- *love* – Psalm 138:2

- *truth* – Psalm 138:2

- *glory* – Psalm 148:13

In the Bible, 'holy' is the word which is most commonly associated with God's name; this, therefore, is a primary description of God's nature. For example, Psalm 33:21; 103:1; 105:3; Ezekiel 36:21 & 39:7.

Psalm 33:21 ☐
103:1 ☐
105:3 ☐

Ezekiel 36:21 ☐
39:7 ☐

The Old Testament underlines the truth that God's name reveals his nature by suggesting that his name can be:

- *blasphemed* – Isaiah 52:5

Isaiah 52:5 ☐

- *polluted* – Jeremiah 34:16

Jeremiah 34:16 ☐

- *profaned* – Proverbs 30:9

Proverbs 30:9 ☐

On the other hand, God's people can, for example,

- *love the name* – Psalm 5:11

Psalm 5:11 ☐

- *praise the name* – Joel 2:26

Joel 2:26 ☐

- *walk in the name* – Micah 4:5

Micah 4:5 ☐

- *think on the name* – Malachi 3:16

Malachi 3:16 ☐

- *wait on the name* – Psalm 52:9

Psalm 52:9 ☐
54:6 ☐

- *thank the name* – Psalm 54:6

- *fear the name* – Malachi 4:2

Malachi 4:2 ☐

- *call on the name* – Psalm 99:6

Psalm 99:6 ☐

- *proclaim the name* – Isaiah 12:4

Isaiah 12:4 ☐

- *bless the name* – Psalm 113:1–2

Psalm 113:1–2 ☐

The name demonstrates the presence of God

Some people today wonder what the difference is between 'calling on the name of God' and 'calling on God'.

In the Bible, 'the name' also demonstrates the *active presence* of a person in the fullness of their revealed nature. For example, in 1 Kings 18:24, Elijah proposed a contest between 'names': the reality of the deities had to be demonstrated by their present personal action.

1 Kings 18:24 ☐

The same idea is expressed when 'the name' refers to God's reputation. When God acts 'for his name's sake', he intervenes out of regard for his reputation – for example, Psalm 79:9–10 and Ezekiel 36:21–23. If God's name is implicated, he is personally involved, and he will take personal action – as in Exodus 34:14.

Psalm 79:9–10 ☐
Ezekiel 36:21–23 ☐
Exodus 34:14 ☐

Numbers 6:27 teaches that imparting a divine blessing involves placing God's name on someone – we consider this in Part Ten of *Ministry in the Spirit*. This means that blessing is imparting the active presence of God in the fullness of his revealed character.

The New Testament often speaks about baptising 'in the name' – as in Acts 2:38 & 10:48. In Part Ten of *Glory in the Church*, we note that baptism rests completely on the authority of God, and is spiritually effective only through his personal presence and activity.

The shared name

Throughout history, the giving of a name by one person to another has demonstrated the joining of those people together. Isaiah 4:1 shows that a wife received her husband's name; and Deuteronomy 28:9–10; Isaiah 43:7; 63:19; 65:1 reveal that Israel became the holy people of the holy God because they had been called by his holy name.

Jeremiah 14:9 uses the basis of the shared name for an appeal to God to save Israel. And Jeremiah 15:16 reveals that the shared name is the foundation of the prophet's personal fellowship with God.

In the Old Testament, God's name is also shared with:

- *Jerusalem* – Jeremiah 25:29; Daniel 9:18

- *the temple* – Jeremiah 32:34

- *the ark* – 2 Samuel 6:2

This sharing of the divine name demonstrates a genuine closeness with the holy nature and presence of God himself. It should be clear that this must have considerable implications for Christian believers.

The New Testament teaches that believers are baptised 'into the name': we see this, for example, in Matthew 28:19; Acts 8:16 & 1 Corinthians 1:13–15. This idea is underlined in James 2:7, and suggests the ideas of union, passing into new ownership, loyalty and fellowship.

If God has given us his own name, it means that we must share both his divine nature *and* his divine presence. As we consider the detail of God's name, we must never forget that this is the name into which we have been baptised. The magnificent nature and presence of God is his conversion gift to us all.

THREE 'ROOT' NAMES

There are three basic *root* names of God. All his other divine names are established on one or more of these three *root* names.

1.   *Elohim*

In the Old Testament, God is identified over 2,500 times by the Hebrew word *Elohim*. In most English versions of the Bible, *Elohim* is simply translated as 'God'. We see this, for example, in Genesis 1:1–2.

It is impossible to know exactly what *Elohim* originally meant, but it is clearly associated with the idea of 'might', 'majesty' and 'strength'; and we can say that it points to absolute, unqualified, unlimited energy.

In Hebrew, *Elohim* is a plural word, yet it always takes a singular verb. To follow this literally today, we would have to say, 'God, they is strong': modern versions of the Bible reflect this in passages like Genesis 1:26. Interestingly, although cognate forms of *Elohim* are found in other Semitic languages, they are always in the singular. This means that the Old Testament makes a unique point in using *Elohim* as it does, and so hints at God's 'one, but more-than-one' nature right from the first chapter of the Bible.

El, a shortened form of *Elohim*, is sometimes used, as in Psalm 19:1, and this is usually translated as 'the mighty one'. *Eloah*, the singular form of *Elohim*, is used in Deuteronomy 32:15–17.

Throughout the Old Testament, particular aspects of God's all-strong, all-mighty, all-majestic nature are revealed by adding Hebrew words to either *Elohim* or *El*. We see, for example, that God is:

- *Elohim Qodesh* – the holy, Joshua 24:19; Isaiah 57:15
- *Elohim Tsur Yesha* – the rock of salvation, 2 Samuel 22:47
- *Elohim Tsur Israel* – the rock of Israel, 2 Samuel 23:3
- *Elohim Maoz* – the strength, Psalm 43:2
- *Elohim Melek* – the king, Psalm 44:4
- *Elohim Olam* – the everlasting, Isaiah 40:28
- *Elohim Erets* – the God of the whole earth, Isaiah 54:5

Genesis 1:1–2 ☐ / Genesis 1:26 ☐ / Psalm 19:1 ☐ / Deuteronomy 32:15–17 ☐ / Joshua 24:19 ☐ / Isaiah 57:15 ☐ / 2 Samuel 22:47 ☐ / 23:3 ☐ / Psalm 43:2 ☐ / 44:4 ☐ / Isaiah 40:28 ☐ / 54:5 ☐

- *Elohim Magen* – the shield, Psalm 84:9
- *Elohim Machseh Metsudah* – the refuge and fortress, Psalm 91:2
- *Elohim Emeth* – the truth, Jeremiah 10:10
- *El Elyon* – the most high, Genesis 14:19
- *El Roi* – the all-seeing, Genesis 16:13
- *El Shaddai* – the almighty, Genesis 17:1
- *El Kanna* – the jealous, Exodus 20:5
- *El Channum Rachum* – the gracious and merciful, Nehemiah 9:31
- *El Gibbur* – the mighty, Nehemiah 9:32
- *El Aman* – the faithful, Deuteronomy 7:9
- *El Emunah* – the reliable, Deuteronomy 32:4
- *El Chai* – the living, Joshua 3:10
- *El Deah* – the all-knowing, 1 Samuel 2:3
- *El Yeshua* – the salvation, Psalm 68:19
- *El Moshaoth* – the deliverer, Psalm 68:20
- *El Asah Pele* – the wonder worker, Psalm 77:14
- *El Shamayim* – the heavenly, Psalm 136:26
- *El Tsaddiq* – the just, Isaiah 45:21

The *Elohim* root is inherent in all these names. So, for example, when God is named in Psalm 68:20 as *El Yeshua*, as the God of salvation, it means that his salvation is packed with strength and might – it is an absolute, unqualified, unlimited, all-powerful salvation.

And when Psalm 77:14 identifies him as *El Asah Pele*, as the God who does wonders, it is explicitly revealing that his wonder-working strength is absolute – without any qualifications or limits.

2.   *Yahweh*

Yahweh is the common name of God, and we can consider it to be his first name, or his personal name. It is used over 6,800 times in the Old Testament, from Genesis 2:4 to Malachi 4:5.

In older versions of the Bible, *Yahweh* is translated with capital letters as 'LORD' or 'GOD'. In most modern translations, however, it appears simply as 'Yahweh' to stress that this is God's personal name.

Yahweh is an ambiguous form of the verb 'to be', and can mean 'I am who I am', or 'I was who I was', or 'I will be who I will be'. This name is clearly hinted at in Revelation 4:8.

Yahweh is singular, and is the name which God used when he revealed himself to Moses in Exodus 3:14 & 6:2–6. These verses show that it is God's most basic nature to become whatever his people need, in order to meet their need.

This idea is plainly seen in Jesus' 'I am' sayings in John 6:35, 51; 8:12; 10:7, 9; 10:11, 14; 11:25; 14:6; 15:1–5.

God is frequently called *Yahweh Elohim*, LORD God, and this wraps together his absolute power and his personal will, his plurality and his oneness, in one divine being. We see this, for example, in Genesis 3:1; 1 Kings 8:15 & Micah 1:2.

As with *Elohim*, several aspects of God's nature are highlighted by joining different Hebrew words to *Yahweh*. So, for example, God is named as the LORD who:

- *Yahweh Yireh* – provides, Genesis 22:14

- *Yahweh Rapha* – heals, Exodus 15:26

- *Yahweh Nissi* – is a battle ensign, Exodus 17:15–16

- *Yahweh M'qaddishkhem* – sanctifies, Exodus 31:13

- *Yahweh Shalom* – brings peace, Judges 6:24

- *Yahweh Sabaoth* – possesses armies, 1 Samuel 1:3

- *Yahweh Rohi* – is a shepherd, Psalm 23:1

- *Yahweh Tsidkenu* – is righteousness, Jeremiah 23:6

- *Yahweh Shammah* – is there, Ezekiel 48:35

3. *Adonai*

Adonai is by far the least common of the three root names of God. It is used about 350 times in the Old Testament, and is always translated into English as 'Lord' – as in Isaiah 6:1.

Adonai points to God's unique authority and shows that he is 'the one who should be obeyed'. In Israel, slaves, wives and subjects used *Adonai* to identify and address their masters, husbands and kings. *Adonai*, therefore, was the natural name for them to use when they were speaking to, or about, their God.

In the Old Testament, *Adonai* is often linked with either *Yahweh* or *Elohim*. For example:

- *Adonai Yahweh* appears about 200 times, and is translated as 'Lord GOD' – as in Genesis 15:2 & Ezekiel 2:4

- *Adonai* is joined to *Elohim* in about fifteen places, and is translated as 'Lord God' – as in Daniel 9:3

- *Adonai*, *Yahweh* and *Elohim* appear together only in Amos 3:13 and 2 Samuel 7:28, where David testifies that 'O Lord GOD, you are God': we can paraphrase this as, 'O my ruler *Yahweh*, you are the all-powerful God'

The root names

We can say that *Elohim* generally points to God's transcendent power, that *Yahweh* usually suggests his immanent, personal presence and will, and that *Adonai* normally refers to his unique authority over men and women.

The Old Testament passages which name God only as *Elohim* tend to focus on his 'beyond-everything' nature – on the abstract, cosmic dimensions of his character. In these passages, he is seen to be the God of heaven and earth who speaks to people mainly through dreams and messengers.

The passages which identify God as *Yahweh* tend to stress the 'with-us' aspects of his nature. It is *Yahweh* who speaks with people in person, who personally meets their needs, and who is clearly Israel's own national God.

And the passages which address God just as *Adonai* focus on the personal relationship that people enjoyed with their Lord – with their owner, spouse and king. Time and again, men and women call God *'my Adonai'*. He may be all-powerful and beyond-everything; he is undoubtedly personal and self-contained; but he is also *'my* Lord'.

Genesis 15:2 ☐

Ezekiel 2:4 ☐

Daniel 9:3 ☐

Amos 3:13 ☐

2 Samuel 7:28 ☐

FOUR *'TRUNK'* NAMES

We have considered many of the scriptural names of God which are founded on *Elohim* and *Yahweh*. Most of these names appear only once or twice each in the Old Testament.

Four of them, however, are used with great frequency; and we can think of them as '*trunk* names growing from the *root* names'. These names reveal fundamental sides of God's nature and character.

1.   *Yahweh Sabaoth* – the 'powerful' God

God is called *Yahweh Sabaoth* about 200 times in the Bible, and this is usually translated in most English versions as 'the LORD of Hosts'.

This name indicates that God is the personal leader of a large and powerful heavenly army. It is a military name which demonstrates that God is a great leader. It reveals the side of his nature which fights battles, defeats enemies and establishes a kingdom.

This name is used most often by King David, as in 1 Samuel 17:45, and appears most frequently in the books of Samuel, Kings, Chronicles, Psalms, and in the early prophets who ministered when Israel and Judah were ruled by kings.

We see this name, for example, in 2 Samuel 5:10; 6:2, 18; 1 Kings 18:15; 1 Chronicles 11:9; Psalm 24:10; 46:7; 84:3; 89:8; Isaiah 1:24; 6:3; 10:26; 13:13; 24:23; 29:6; 47:4; 51:15; Jeremiah 10:16; 32:18; 51:14; Hosea 12:5; Nahum 2:13; Zephaniah 2:10; Haggai 2:7–9; Zechariah 9:15; 13:7 and Malachi 3:10.

Many other names express similar aspects of God's military character. For example:

- *strength* – Psalm 18:1; 59:9, 17; 81:1; 92:15; 116:5; 129:4; Isaiah 12:2; Jeremiah 16:19; Habakkuk 3:19

- *mighty One* – Genesis 49:24; Psalm 132:2; Isaiah 49:26

- *warrior* – Exodus 15:3; Zephaniah 3:17

- *war banner* – Exodus 17:15

- *triumphant and terrible* – Deuteronomy 10:17

1 Samuel 17:45 ☐
2 Samuel 5:10 ☐
1 Kings 18:15 ☐
1 Chronicles 11:9 ☐
Psalm 24:10 ☐
46:7 ☐
84:3 ☐
Isaiah 1:24 ☐
6:3 ☐
51:15 ☐
Jeremiah 10:16 ☐
32:18 ☐
51:14 ☐
Hosea 12:5 ☐
Nahum 2:13 ☐
Zephaniah 2:10 ☐
Haggai 2:7–9 ☐
Zechariah 9:15 ☐
13:7 ☐
Malachi 3:10 ☐

Psalm 18:1 ☐
59:9, 17 ☐
Isaiah 12:2 ☐
Jeremiah 16:19 ☐
Habakkuk 3:19 ☐
Genesis 49:24 ☐
Psalm 132:2 ☐
Exodus 15:3 ☐
Zephaniah 3:17 ☐
Exodus 17:15 ☐
Deuteronomy 10:17 ☐

- *marching sword* – Deuteronomy 33:29

- *lord of the battle* – 1 Samuel 17:47

- *glory and power* – 1 Chronicles 16:28

- *valiant* – Psalm 24:8

- *retribution* – Jeremiah 51:56

- *deliverer* – Psalm 18:2

2.   *El Elyon* – the 'protecting' God

El Elyon is generally translated as 'the Most High', and it reveals the side of God's character which serves his people by strongly protecting them from all kinds of harm. It suggests infinite height and strength.

This name is first used in Genesis 14:18 in connection with Melchizedek, who was 'a priest of God Most High', and is then used about another fifty times in the Old Testament.

The name *El Elyon* is used, for example, in Genesis 14:18–22; Numbers 24:16; Deuteronomy 32:8; Psalm 7:17; 21:7; 57:2; 82:6; 92:1 & Daniel 7:15–27.

Although *El Elyon* is the least common of the four 'trunk' names, so many of God's other names are linked to this aspect of his nature that 'protection' is the scriptural characteristic which is most commonly associated with God's name and nature. We see this in these names:

- *shield* – Deuteronomy 33:29

- *support* – 2 Samuel 22:19

- *rock* – 2 Samuel 23:3

- *fortress* – Psalm 18:2

- *saviour* – Psalm 24:5

- *refuge* – Psalm 31:4

- *protector* – Psalm 31:23

- *shelter* – Psalm 43:2

- *citadel* – Psalm 59:9–17

- *strong tower* – Psalm 61:3

- *safety* – Psalm 61:2–6

- *battlement* – Psalm 84:11

- *sanctuary* – Isaiah 8:13–14

- *defender* –Isaiah 51:22

- *stronghold* – Jeremiah 16:19

3.   *El Qodesh* – the 'perfect' God

God is named as *El Qodesh* or *Qodesh* about sixty times in the Old Testament, and this is usually translated into English as 'the Holy One' or 'the Holy One of Israel'.

God revealed this holy, 'set apart', side of his nature in Leviticus 11:44–45, and this basic name demonstrates that God is set apart from creation by his eternal, uncreated nature and moral perfection. *El Qodesh* suggests that God may not be approached by those who are morally flawed.

This name appears most often in Leviticus, Psalms, Isaiah and Ezekiel, for example: Leviticus 19:2; 20:26; 21:8; Psalm 71:22; 89:18; Isaiah 1:4; 12:6; 29:23; 30:15; 43:3; 47:4; 49:7; 57:15; Jeremiah 51:5; Ezekiel 39:7 and Hosea 11:9.

We see different aspects of God's 'set-apart-ness' and 'absolute moral perfection' in these names:

- *judge* – Genesis 18:25

- *sanctifier* –Exodus 31:13

- *cloud* – Numbers 9:15–21

- *consuming fire* – Deuteronomy 4:24

- *faithful* – Deuteronomy 32:4

- *jealous* – Joshua 24:19

- *heavenly* – 2 Chronicles 20:6

- *arbiter* – Psalm 7:8

- *righteous* – Psalm 11:7

Psalm 61:2–6 ☐
84:11 ☐

Isaiah 8:13–14 ☐
51:22 ☐

Jeremiah 16:19 ☐

Leviticus
11:44–45 ☐
19:2 ☐
20:26 ☐
21:8 ☐

Psalm 71:22 ☐
89:18 ☐

Isaiah 1:4 ☐
12:6 ☐
29:23 ☐
30:15 ☐
43:3 ☐
47:4 ☐
49:7 ☐
57:15 ☐

Jeremiah 51:5 ☐

Ezekiel 39:7 ☐

Hosea 11:9 ☐

Genesis 18:25 ☐

Exodus 31:13 ☐

Numbers 9:15–21 ☐

Deuteronomy
4:24 ☐
32:4 ☐

Joshua 24:19 ☐

2 Chronicles 20:6 ☐

Psalm 7:8 ☐
11:7 ☐

- *king of glory* – Psalm 24:8–10

- *truth* – Psalm 31:5

- *illustrious and majestic* – Psalm 76:4

- *hidden* – Isaiah 45:15

- *just* – Isaiah 45:21

The perfect side of God can be seen particularly clearly in *Yahweh's* revelation of himself in Exodus 34:6. We can think of this verse as God's 'amplified' name, and it is fundamental to the Jewish and Christian understanding of God.

Several forms of this amplified name appear throughout the Old Testament – for example, 2 Chronicles 30:9; Psalm 86:15; 103:8; 116:5; Nehemiah 9:17, 31; Joel 2:13; Jonah 4:2 & Nahum 1:2.

4.   *El Shaddai* – the 'providing' God

In most older versions of the Bible, *El Shaddai* is normally translated as 'the Almighty'. It is difficult, however to justify this translation by the context in which it is usually used in the Old Testament.

It is not possible to know the original meaning of *Shaddai,* or its derivation. Many teachers think that it comes from the Assyrian word for 'mountain', and use this to justify 'Almighty'. Others, however, argue that it is derived from the Aramiac word for 'to pour'; while a few point to *Shaddai*'s similarity to the Hebrew word for 'breast'.

The Septuagint – the Greek version of the Old Testament – translated *El Shaddai* as 'the Sufficient', and this makes excellent sense when we see that *El Shaddai* is almost always used in the Old Testament in the context of God's extravagant covenant provision.

This 'trunk' name reveals God as all-providing. It was first used in Genesis 17:1–5, when God introduced himself to Abraham and covenanted to provide him with a large family. It is used about fifty times in the Old Testament, mainly in books like Genesis, Ruth and Job which focus on the issue of God's covenant provision.

We see *El Shaddai* in, for example: Genesis 28:3; 35:11; 43:14; 48:3; 49:25; Exodus 6:3; Numbers 24:4; 24:16; Ruth 1:20–21; Job 5:17; 8:5; 21:20; 22:17; 27:10–13; 31:2; 33:4; Psalm 91:1; Ezekiel 1:24; 10:5.

The providing side of God's nature is also seen in these names:

- *provider* – Genesis 22:14
- *lamp* – 2 Samuel 22:29
- *maker* – Job 4:17
- *goodness* – Psalm 16:2
- *cup* – Psalm 16:5
- *counsellor* – Psalm 16:7
- *light* – Psalm 27:1
- *comforter* – Isaiah 51:12
- *fountain* – Jeremiah 17:13

Genesis 22:14 ☐
2 Samuel 22:29 ☐
Job 4:17 ☐
Psalm 16:2–7 ☐
27:1 ☐
Isaiah 51:12 ☐
Jeremiah 17:13 ☐

TWELVE *'BRANCH'* NAMES

We have seen that there are three *root* names of God which appear thousands of times in the Old Testament and which stress his transcendence, immanence and authority. And we have examined the four *trunk* names which reveal the fundamental sides of his character.

We have also noted about ninety names which are linked to these seven either by language or context: these highlight distinct aspects of God's nature, and most appear only once or twice in the Bible.

There are twelve divine names, however, which each appear about a dozen times. We can think of these as 'branch names which stem from the *trunks* and *roots*'. These names highlight important scriptural aspects of God's nature. We should recognise and remember the special emphasis that the Bible gives to them. They are:

- *God of heaven and earth* – Genesis 24:7; Joshua 2:11
- *judge* – Judges 11:27; Psalm 7:11
- *king* – Psalm 47:6; Jeremiah 10:10
- *God of your father* – Genesis 46:3; 1 Chronicles 28:9

Genesis 24:7 ☐
Joshua 2:11 ☐
Judges 11:27 ☐
Psalm 7:11 ☐
47:6 ☐
Jeremiah 10:10 ☐
Genesis 46:3 ☐
1 Chronicles 28:9 ☐

- *maker* – Isaiah 22:11; Jeremiah 10:16
- *rock* – Psalm 18:2; 62:2
- *jealous* – Exodus 34:14; Nahum 1:2
- *God of Israel* – Exodus 5:1; Judges 5:3
- *shield* – 2 Samuel 22:31; Psalm 115:9–11
- *saviour* – Isaiah 43:3, 21
- *strength* – Psalm 59:9; Habakkuk 3:19
- *living God* – 1 Samuel 17:26–36; Daniel 6:20–26

God is also often named as the God of a particular person. This underlines the truth that the revelation of God is essentially relational: it is personal not propositional. For example:

- *the God of Abraham* – Psalm 47:9
- *the God of Jacob* – Psalm 20:1
- *the God of David* – Isaiah 38:5
- *the God of Elijah* – 2 Kings 2:14

OTHER NAMES

There are also about 200 names and titles of God which appear only once or twice in the Bible, and point to particular aspects of God's nature. There is not enough space to list them all here, but we can note each one when we read them in the Scriptures – and we can then ask God to reveal that side of his nature to us in our experience.

Here is a small selection from the 'minor' names of God:

- *the all-seeing God* – Genesis 16:13
- *the everlasting God* – Genesis 21:33
- *the fear of Isaac* – Genesis 31:42
- *the one God* – Deuteronomy 6:4
- *the peace-bringing God* – Judges 6:24

- *the all-knowing God* – 1 Samuel 2:3

- *the ruler over all* – 1 Chronicles 29:11

- *the guardian of my rights* – Psalm 4:1

- *the shepherd* – Psalm 23:1

- *the God of my life* – Psalm 42:8

- *the God of my joy* – Psalm 43:4

- *the source of my hope* – Psalm 62:5

- *the rider of the clouds* – Psalm 68:4

- *the father of orphans and defender of widows* – Psalm 68:5

- *the all-hearing God* – Psalm 77:1

- *the listening God* – Psalm 116:1

- *the restorer of Jerusalem* – Psalm 147:2

- *the giver of wisdom* – Proverbs 2:6

- *the oil poured out* – Song of Songs 1:3

- *the first and with the last* – Isaiah 41:4

- *the revealer of mysteries* – Daniel 2:29

- *the ancient of days* – Daniel 7:9

In this chapter, we have developed a picture of God's name by using the metaphor of a tree. We have thought of 'root', 'trunk' and 'branch' names, and have categorised the names according to the number of times that they are used. This helps us to appreciate the different biblical emphases, and to grasp that some popular names (like, for example, 'the all-healing God') occur rarely, while other less well-known names (like 'the rock') are more common. We must remember, however, that:

- *God's eternal, infinite and immortal nature means that he is all his names, all the time.*

- *The different names introduce us to different facets of his nature, but the phrase 'the name of God' encapsulates them all.*

- *All the names apply equally and fully to the Father, the Son and the Spirit. All three persons share the same name and nature.*

1 Samuel 2:3 ☐

1 Chronicles
    29:11 ☐

Psalm 4:1 ☐
    23:1 ☐
    42:8 ☐
    43:4 ☐
    62:5 ☐
    68:4–5 ☐
    77:1 ☐
    116:1 ☐
    147:2 ☐

Proverbs 2:6 ☐

Song of Songs
    1:3 ☐

Isaiah 41:4 ☐

Daniel 2:29 ☐
    7:9 ☐

Descriptions

A series of astonishingly beautiful descriptions of God are scattered throughout the Scriptures, and they are all set in the context of God's relationships with his people. If we wanted to stretch the 'tree' metaphor to its limit, we could think of them as 'flowers' adorning 'the tree of life'!

While these are not actual names of God, they are wonderful descriptions of his nature in action – as experienced by his people.

If we are hungry to know God, and to know him in the fullness of his holy name and nature, we will read and meditate on all these passages. They reveal what God is like, and what he does for his people.

Exodus 15:11; 34:6–7; Leviticus 10:3; Numbers 6:24–27; Deuteronomy 4:35–39; 32:3–4; 32:39–41; 1 Samuel 2:6–10; 2 Samuel 22; 2 Kings 19:15–19; 1 Chronicles 16:8–36; 29:10–19; 2 Chronicles 14:10–11; 20:6; Nehemiah 9:5–38; Job 9:1–13; 11:7; 36:22 – 37:24; 38:1 – 39:30; Psalm 36:6–9; 86:15–16; 89:7–8; 91:1–2, 14–16; 103:1–6; 104:24–25, 34; 136; 145; 146:7–10; Jeremiah 32:17–20; Daniel 7:9–14 and Habakkuk 3:1–19.

PART THREE

the fatherhood of god

In Part Two, we saw that God's 'name' dominates the Old Testament revelation about God; now we will see that the idea of God's 'fatherhood' fills the New Testament.

From Matthew 2:15 through to Revelation 14:1, the understanding of God as essentially 'Father' shapes and affects every part of the New Testament. The Old Testament names God as 'Father' only four times, but he is called 'Father' in the New Testament over 250 times.

THE FATHER IN THE OLD TESTAMENT

In the past, some Bible teachers over-emphasised the differences between the Old and New Testaments, and overlooked the presence of God's 'fatherhood' in the Old Testament.

But the Old Testament often compares God's relationship with Israel as a whole, and with individual Jews, to that of a father. We see this for example, in Deuteronomy 1:31; 8:5 and Psalm 103:13.

Matthew 2:15 □
Revelation 14:1 □

Deuteronomy
1:31 □
8:5 □
Psalm 103:13 □

More importantly, the Old Testament clearly presents God as:

- *the Father of Israel* – Deuteronomy 32:6; Jeremiah 3:4, 19; 31:9

- *the Father of individual Israelites* – Isaiah 63:16; 64:8; Malachi 2:10

The Old Testament gives the corollaries of these statements an even greater emphasis. It often states, for example, that:

- *Israel is 'God's Son'* – Exodus 4:22–23; Hosea 11:1; Jeremiah 3:19; 31:20; Psalm 89:27

- *individual Jews are his 'children'* – Deuteronomy 14:1.

The Old Testament also prophesies, in Isaiah 9:6, that the Messiah will be 'the Mighty God and the Everlasting Father'. This idea of 'messianic fatherhood' can be seen, for example, in Psalms 2 & 89. (We return to this in Part Five.)

This means we can say that God's fatherhood is present in the Old Testament, but that it is merely one divine attribute among many. God's fatherhood was not basic to Jewish understanding, it was merely part of their general sense of privilege at being the 'Chosen People'. As we will see, God's fatherhood is developed in the New Testament.

GOD IN THE NEW TESTAMENT

The New Testament shares the same basic understanding of God as the Old Testament, but it focuses on fewer aspects of his nature.

God is often called 'the God of Abraham, Isaac and Jacob', and this shows that God's nature in the New Testament is the same as when he dealt in covenant grace with the patriarchs. We see this, for example, in Matthew 8:11; 22:32; Luke 20:37; Acts 3:13; 22:14.

And God is also called 'the Alpha and Omega' in Revelation 1:8 and 21:6 – a name which stresses the continuity of God's nature. As we have seen, because God is eternal, infinite and immortal, he must – by definition – be unchanging.

The Creator

The New Testament stresses that God is the creator of heaven and earth, the maker of all things. We see this, for example, in Matthew 19:4; Mark 10:6; 13:19; Acts 14:15; 17:24, 29; Romans 1:20; 11:36; 1 Corinthians 8:6; 11:12; Ephesians 3:9 and Revelation 4:11.

The New Testament also reminds us that creation is not co-eternal with the Creator. Passages like John 17:5, 24, Ephesians 1:4 and 1 Peter 1:20 illustrate the New Testament belief that God exists apart from the material reality of creation.

The King

Jesus taught more about the kingdom than any other topic, and this implicitly points to God as king. We consider the kingdom of God in *The Rule of God* in this *Sword of the Spirit* series.

Acts 4:24 shows that kingship, or sovereignty, stems from creatorship: the God who creates has a right to direct. And Romans 9:19–21 demonstrates that kingship is part of God's creative activity.

God's kingship is also seen in the many New Testament references to:

- *God's lordship* – Matthew 4:7, 10

- *God's throne* – Matthew 5:34; 23:22; Revelation 4:2; 5:1; 20:11; 21:5

- *God's sovereignty* – 1 Corinthians 2:6–8; 15:24; Romans 8:37–39; Colossians 2:15; 1 Timothy 6:15; Revelation 6:10

- *God's majesty* – Hebrews 1:3; 8:1; 12:2; 1 Peter 3:22

The Judge

The concept of God as king is closely linked to that of God as judge.

The absolute certainty of God's judgement is the basic assumption behind John's preaching in Matthew 3:7–12; Luke 3:7–9, and Jesus' teaching in Matthew 7:1–2; 11:22–24; 12:36–37; Luke 18:7; John 8:16.

The idea of God as Judge can also be seen, for example, in Romans 2:16; 3:6 and 14:10.

Matthew 19:4 ☐
Mark 10:6 ☐
13:19 ☐
Acts 14:15 ☐
17:24, 29 ☐
Romans 1:20 ☐
11:36 ☐
1 Corinthians 8:6 ☐
11:12 ☐
Ephesians 3:9 ☐
Revelation 4:11 ☐
John 17:5, 24 ☐
Ephesians 1:4 ☐
1 Peter 1:20 ☐
Acts 4:24 ☐
Romans 9:19–21 ☐
Matthew 4:7, 10 ☐
5:34 ☐
23:22 ☐
Revelation 4:2 ☐
5:1 ☐
20:11 ☐
21:5 ☐
1 Corinthians 2:6–8 ☐
15:24 ☐
Romans 8:37–39 ☐
Colossians 2:15 ☐
1 Timothy 6:15 ☐
Revelation 6:10 ☐
Hebrews 1:3 ☐
8:1 ☐
12:2 ☐
1 Peter 3:22 ☐
Matthew 7:1–2 ☐
11:22–24 ☐
12:36–37 ☐
Luke 18:7 ☐
John 8:16 ☐
Romans 2:16 ☐
3:6 ☐
14:10 ☐

The Saviour

Although the divine title 'Saviour' is generally applied to Jesus in the New Testament, it is also given – as in the Old Testament – to God.

God is named as Saviour in Luke 1:47; 1 Timothy 2:3; Titus 2:10, 13; 3:4; Jude 1:25. And the theme of God saving his people is central to the New Testament, and fundamental to our Christian understanding and experience of God.

The Father

From the beginning of the New Testament to the end, the idea of God as Father is presented so frequently that his fatherhood has become a central feature of Christianity.

In fact, God is not merely identified as 'Father' over 250 times in the New Testament, he is called 'Father' in every book except one.

The Father is mentioned in, for example, Matthew 5:16; Mark 14:36; Luke 11:2; John 14:8; Acts 2:33; Romans 1:7; 1 Corinthians 8:6; 2 Corinthians 1:3; Galatians 4:6; Ephesians 4:6; Philippians 4:20; Colossians 1:12; 1 Thessalonians 3:11; 2 Thessalonians 2:16; 1 Timothy 1:2; 2 Timothy 1:2; Titus 1:4; Philemon 1:3; Hebrews 1:5; James 1:17; 1 Peter 1:2; 2 Peter 1:17; 1 John 3:1; 2 John 1:4; Jude 1:1 & Revelation 3:5.

THE FATHERHOOD OF GOD

It is Jesus who presents the fatherhood of God with most clarity. None of God's names was more constantly used by Jesus than 'Father'; and no other divine name seems to have so dominated his thoughts – both for his disciples and himself.

Through Jesus, we learn that fatherhood is not one divine attribute among many, it is the central attitude which colours and shapes all the rest.

Time and again, Jesus bases his arguments and teaching on the fact of God's fatherhood: this is the foundation which lies below many of his deductions and much of his teaching. We see this, for example, in passages like Matthew 6:26, 32; 7:9–11 and 10:29–31.

Matthew 6:26, 32 ☐
7:9–11 ☐
10:29–31 ☐

We can say that the Old Testament presents God as *Yahweh Elohim* – as 'one, but more-than-one', as 'full of will and power', as 'perfect, protecting, providing, powerful'; and that Jesus then pulls *all* these aspects together and into focus, and reveals God as essentially Father.

In the New Testament, God is everything that he has been revealed to be in the Old Testament – and is still sometimes referred to by the phrase, 'the name' – but now he is finally revealed as 'the Father God'.

Just as the phrase 'the name' in the Old Testament encapsulates *every* revelation of God's nature to Israel, so 'Father' encapsulates in the New Testament every manifestation and experience of God in Israel *plus* everything which is taught by and seen in Jesus.

In his teaching, Jesus presents three aspects of God's fatherhood.

1.   God is the universal Father of all humanity

Jesus makes it clear that God is the father of all people and all nations. God's fatherhood is not restricted to a chosen few. His fatherly attributes are displayed even to 'the unthankful and the evil'. We see this, for example, in Matthew 5:45 and Luke 6:35.

Matthew 5:45 ☐

Luke 6:35 ☐

2.   God is the redeeming Father of all believers

Jesus also makes it plain that, in some special sense, God is the Father of believers and disciples. Throughout the New Testament, the father-child relationship between people and God is reserved for believers, and is the result of God's redemptive activity.

We see this, for example, in Matthew 6:9, 32; Romans 8:28 and Hebrews 12:5–7.

Matthew 6:9, 32 ☐
Romans 8:28 ☐
Hebrews 12:5–7 ☐

3.   God is the unique Father of Jesus

Jesus is often described as 'God's only Son', and this points implicitly to God's unique fatherhood of Jesus. Mark 1:11 reports that Jesus' ministry begins with the announcement of his sonship, and this announcement is repeated in Mark 9:7.

Mark 1:11 ☐
9:7 ☐

John 20:17 ☐

Matthew 11:27 ☐

John 10:15–18 ☐
     10:29–30 ☐

Acts 17:28–29 ☐

Romans 8:15–17 ☐

Galatians 4:6 ☐

1 Peter 1:17 ☐

Romans
    11:25–27 ☐

Romans 15:6 ☐

2 Corinthians
    11:31 ☐

Ephesians 1:3 ☐

1 Peter 1:3 ☐

Jesus does not speak of 'our Father' as embracing both himself and his disciples; instead he speaks of 'my Father and your Father' – as in John 20:17. It is this unique aspect of fatherhood which lies behind Jesus' statements in Matthew 11:27 and John 10:15–18, 29–30.

Three aspects of fatherhood

These three distinct aspects of God's fatherhood can also be seen in the rest of the New Testament.

The first aspect is least prominent, but is mentioned in Acts 17:28–29.

The second aspect is seen, for example, in Romans 8:15–17; Galatians 4:6 & 1 Peter 1:17. Although elements of God's fatherhood are reserved for Christians, we must remember that we hold our privileges as children in trust for the rest of the world. Romans 11:25–27 prophesies that the fullness of the Gentiles, and the fullness of Israel, will one day be brought into the family of God.

The third aspect is seen in the many passages, like Romans 15:6; 2 Corinthians 11:31; Ephesians 1:3 & 1 Peter 1:3, which show that God is the unique Father of his unique Son.

As believers, we need to recognise these three aspects of fatherhood.

- *We are called to know the Father generally, as members of humanity, and to trust in his provision and care for his creation.*

- *We are also called to know him personally and intimately, as those have been adopted into his holy family, and to trust in his redemption, grace and hope.*

- *But we cannot know him in exactly the same way as Jesus, for there is an aspect of God's fatherhood which is unique to Jesus.*

OUR FATHER

It is difficult today for us to appreciate just what a radical prayer Jesus taught his disciples to use. We are so familiar with 'the Lord's Prayer' that we consider it 'traditional'. Yet it was a remarkable revelation of God which revolutionised his disciples' understanding.

We have seen that God was known in the Old Testament by the primary names *El Elyon*, *Yahweh Sabaoth*, *El Qodesh* and *El Shaddai* – names which reveal that God is essentially 'Protecting', 'Powerful', 'Perfect' and 'Providing'. Each of these primary aspects of God's nature is addressed in the Lord's Prayer, for example:

Matthew 6:9–13 ☐
Luke 11:2–4 ☐

- 'Do not lead us into temptation, but deliver us from the evil one,' asks for *God's protection*.

- 'Your kingdom come, your will be done,' and 'Yours is the kingdom and the power,' focus on *God's power*.

- 'Hallowed be your name,' and 'Yours is the glory,' address *God's perfection*.

- 'Give us this day our daily bread,' and 'Forgive us our debts,' plead for *God's provision*.

The radical nature of the prayer was not its content, it was its direct approach to 'Our Father' – which was typical of Jesus' attitude to God.

The Lord's Prayer makes it plain that our heavenly Father is *Yahweh Elohim*, is *El Elyon*, *Yahweh Sabaoth*, *El Qodesh*, and *El Shaddai*, is 'the Name', and so on. The Prayer makes it clear not only that the great Creator is 'the' ultimate Father, but also that he is 'our' intimate Father.

The close relationship with God which is assumed by the phrase 'our Father' is even more striking when we note the words which follow. By now, we should be able to appreciate the special resonance of the phrase, 'Hallowed by your *Name*'.

Our Father is not an old friend, he is 'the hallowed Name'; he is the holy unapproachable Name who fills the universe with his presence and is beyond-life, beyond-matter, beyond-space and beyond-time.

We must recognise that the first phrase of the Lord's Prayer is an extraordinary paradox. Jesus beckons us to approach 'our Father', but to approach him knowing that he is 'the Holy Name'.

We can say that the Old Testament painstakingly builds up – level by level, attribute by attribute, book by book – the fullest possible picture of God's nature to awe and inspire us. The full scriptural revelation of God as 'the Name' is almost too magnificent and too terrible to contemplate. But Jesus then comes and teaches that the holy God is actually our very own Father – and he reveals how we can know him.

God is never less than his Old Testament revelation, or in any way different from that revelation. It is merely that Jesus shows us how to understand 'the Name', how to approach 'the Name', and how to live in relationship with 'the Name'. He shows us how to know the Father.

It is vital we appreciate that 'our Father' is 'the Name'. Our intimate relationship with the Father must not diminish our awe in approaching him. We must not reduce the biblical view of God's fatherhood to the level of our human experience of fatherhood. Our earthly relationships with our parents will always be imperfect, but – in God – the perfect pattern of true parenthood is permanently seen.

Ephesians 3:14–15 □

Ephesians 3:14–15 teaches that all human fatherhood comes from God. This means that he is not called Father as a human analogy, as if human fatherhood was the best way of describing God's relationship with believers. Fatherhood is inherent to God's nature, and it exists within humanity only because we have been made in the image of God.

Abba

Mark 14:36 □

Mark 14:36 indicates that Jesus used the Aramaic word *Abba* to address God. This word was originally used by small children when they spoke to their human fathers, but – by New Testament times – it was more generally used by adult Jews to express their familiar relationship with their parents.

Abba is never used in the Old Testament to address God. And its use by Jesus illustrates how his view of God as Father, and his relationship with God as Father, are without formality.

Romans 8:15 □

Galatians 4:6 □

The use of *Abba* in Romans 8:15 and Galatians 4:6 reveals the intimacy and familiarity with 'our Father' which is open to us through the work of the Spirit. We consider this in more detail in Part Five.

Father knows

Matthew 6:32 □

We have seen that the Old Testament identifies God as all-knowing, and Jesus brings this into sharp focus in Matthew 6:32 with his insistence that it is 'your heavenly Father' who knows.

In this passage, Jesus shows that our Father knows all our everyday needs, the small details as well as the big concerns. And he makes it plain that 'our Father' is the great Creator by explaining God's care for his creatures in terms of *fatherhood* rather than *creatorship* – this underlines the concept of God's individual care and concern. We also see this in Matthew 6:26–32 & 10:29–30.

This revelation by Jesus of the all-knowing, all-caring, all-individual Father (who is the all-powerful, all-providing, all-protecting, all-perfect *Yahweh Elohim*) is emphasised throughout the New Testament.

Most of Paul's letters begin with a declaration of the fatherhood of God, and this understanding of God as essentially Father is the basic assumption behind all Paul's teaching. We see this, for example, in 1 Corinthians 1:3; 2 Corinthians 1:3; Galatians 1:3–4; Ephesians 1:2–3; Philippians 1:2; Colossians 1:2–3, and so on.

Matthew 6:26–32 ☐
10:29–30 ☐

1 Corinthians 1:3 ☐

2 Corinthians 1:3 ☐

Galatians 1:3–4 ☐

Ephesians 1:2–3 ☐

Philippians 1:2 ☐

Colossians 1:2–3 ☐

THE FATHER'S ATTRIBUTES

Just as God's nature in the Old Testament is revealed by adding words to his root names, so God's fatherhood in the New Testament is qualified to develop its richness. We see, for example, that he is:

- *the Father, the Lord of heaven and earth* – Matthew 11:25

- *the holy Father* – John 17:11

- *the righteous Father* – John 17:25

- *the Father of Jesus Christ* – 2 Corinthians 1:3

- *the Father of mercies* – 2 Corinthians 1:3

- *the Father of glory* – Ephesians 1:17

- *the Father of spirits* – Hebrews 12:9

- *the Father of lights* – James 1:17

Matthew 11:25 ☐

John 17:11 ☐
17:25 ☐

2 Corinthians 1:3 ☐

Ephesians 1:17 ☐

Hebrews 12:9 ☐

James 1:17 ☐

Once again, we need to recognise that the biblical revelation about God is personal not propositional; relational, not theoretical.

The New Testament does not present abstract truths about God's fatherhood, instead it reveals the Father through his relationships with his children – and especially through his relationship with his only Son.

The New Testament introduces us to the Father so that we can *know him* personally and intimately, and not just know truths 'about' him.

In the context of God's relationships with men and women, the New Testament shows us, for example, what the Father does for his children, how he relates to them, and what he expects from them.

The New Testament demonstrates, for example, that the Father:

- *possesses glory and can be glorified* – Matthew 5:16; Mark 8:38
- *is perfect* – Matthew 5:48
- *gives rewards* – Matthew 6:1
- *sees everything* – Matthew 6:4
- *knows everything* – Matthew 6:8; 1 Peter 1:2
- *forgives* – Matthew 6:14
- *provides* – Matthew 6:26; James 1:17
- *has will* – Matthew 7:21; 18:14
- *responds to prayer* – Matthew 26:53
- *works through baptism* – Matthew 28:19
- *is merciful* – Luke 6:36
- *loves* – John 3:35; 14:23; 1 John 3:1
- *deserves worship* – John 4:21–23
- *works* – John 5:17
- *raises the dead* – John 5:21
- *is the source of life* – John 5:26
- *gives* – John 6:32
- *teaches* – John 8:28
- *is one with Jesus* – John 10:30
- *provides grace and peace* – Romans 1:7
- *should be thanked* – Colossians 1:12
- *disciplines* – Hebrews 12:5–11

Matthew 5:16 ☐

Mark 8:38 ☐

Matthew 5:48 ☐

6:1 ☐

6:4 ☐

6:8 ☐

1 Peter 1:2 ☐

Matthew 6:14 ☐

6:26 ☐

James 1:17 ☐

Matthew 7:21 ☐

18:14 ☐

26:53 ☐

28:19 ☐

Luke 6:36 ☐

John 3:35 ☐

14:23 ☐

1 John 3:1 ☐

John 4:21–23 ☐

5:17 ☐

5:21 ☐

5:26 ☐

6:32 ☐

8:28 ☐

10:30 ☐

Romans 1:7 ☐

Colossians 1:12 ☐

Hebrews 12:5–11 ☐

The New Testament does not define the Father's nature and attributes; instead, it contains a mass of incidents and examples which offer insights into his holy character and actions.

It is not really possible to develop a systematic picture of divine fatherhood, but several main features of the Father's nature are clear:

1.   His glory and power

The glory of God is one the Bible's greatest themes, and we consider what it means in some detail in *Glory in the Church*.

Ephesians 1:17 describes God as the 'Father of glory', and the glory of God is mentioned frequently throughout the New Testament – for example, Luke 9:26; John 17:5; Acts 7:55; Romans 3:23; 5:2; 2 Corinthians 3:18 and 2 Peter 1:17.

The Father is supremely glorious, and Hebrews 1:3 shows that Jesus reflects his glory. This means that Christ presents in his person the *whole* nature of God – his majesty, power, love *and* his fatherhood. This is the 'messianic fatherhood' which is referred to in Old Testament passages like Isaiah 9:6.

The glory of the Father should cause us to respond with awe and worship, and to prepare for his power. Such a glorious being could not be weak, and the phrase 'the power of God' is often used to point to this attribute of the Father.

We see this, for example, in Romans 4:21; 11:23; 1 Corinthians 2:5; 2 Corinthians 6:7; 9:8; 13:4; 2 Timothy 1:8.

2.   His wisdom and will

We have noted the Father's knowledge in Matthew 6:4–8, and 1 Peter 1:2 extends this to include his 'foreknowledge'. The 'beyond-time' nature of God means that he must know the future if he knows the present and past. Passages like Ephesians 1:5 show that this is part of the basic New Testament understanding of God.

If the Father is all-wise and all-knowing, it follows that his will, plans and purposes must, by definition, be perfect. Titus 1:2 states that God never lies, and Hebrews 6:18 stresses that it is impossible for him to be proved false. We consider the Father's will in detail in Part Seven.

Ephesians 1:17 ☐

Luke 9:26 ☐

John 17:5 ☐

Acts 7:55 ☐

Romans 3:23 ☐
5:2 ☐

2 Corinthians
3:18 ☐

2 Peter 1:17 ☐

Hebrews 1:3 ☐

Isaiah 9:6 ☐

Romans 4:21 ☐
11:23 ☐

1 Corinthians 2:5 ☐

2 Corinthians 6:7 ☐
9:8 ☐
13:4 ☐

2 Timothy 1:8 ☐

Matthew 6:4–8 ☐

1 Peter 1:2 ☐

Ephesians 1:5 ☐

Titus 1:2 ☐

Hebrews 6:18 ☐

3.　　His absolute holiness

We have seen that holiness is the most emphasised quality of God's name; and John 17:11 identifies God as 'holy Father'. This suggests that Jesus was particularly conscious of his father's holiness when facing the cross.

The New Testament always makes it plain that the Father's character and actions are totally holy. He is completely set-apart; his purity is absolute.

4.　　His righteousness and wrath

Jesus identifies God as 'righteous Father' in John 17:25, and the Father's righteousness is basic to the whole plan of salvation. We consider this more fully in *Salvation by Grace* in this series.

- Romans 1:17 & 3:21–22 insist that God's righteousness has been revealed.

- Jesus' demands for righteousness in Matthew 5:20 & 6:33 presuppose the Father's righteousness.

- Romans 10:3; 2 Corinthians 5:21; Ephesians 4:24 & Philippians 3:9 show that God is perfectly righteous.

- The context of John 17:25 suggests that God's righteousness was vitally important to Jesus when he was contemplating the Father's judgement.

It is clear that an absolutely righteous Father must judge in a perfectly righteous manner – which means that God is impartial and has no favourites. This was a difficult idea for the Jews to accept. Passages like Acts 10:34; Romans 2:11; 3:5; Galatians 2:6; Hebrews 6:10 & 1 Peter 1:17 describe the early church's developing appreciation of God's impartiality.

The Father's wrath is an important aspect of his righteousness: we see this, for example, in Romans 1:18; 5:9; 12:19; 13:5; Ephesians 5:6; Colossians 3:6; & 1 Thessalonians 5:9. We can say that God's wrath expresses the revulsion of his absolute holiness to all that is not holy.

The book of Revelation presents God's wrath particularly clearly, and sets it in the context of God's final judgement – as in 6:16:14:10, 19; 15:1, 7; 16:1; 19:15.

Sidebar references:

John 17:11 ☐

John 17:25 ☐

Romans 1:17 ☐
　　3:21–22 ☐
　　10:3 ☐

Matthew 5:20 ☐
　　6:33 ☐

2 Corinthians
　　5:21 ☐

Ephesians 4:24 ☐

Philippians 3:9 ☐

Acts 10:34 ☐

Romans 2:11 ☐
　　3:5 ☐

Galatians 2:6 ☐

Hebrews 6:10 ☐

1 Peter 1:17 ☐

Romans 1:18 ☐
　　5:9 ☐
　　12:19 ☐
　　13:5 ☐

Ephesians 5:6 ☐

Colossians 3:6 ☐

1 Thessalonians
　　5:9 ☐

Revelation 6:16 ☐
　　14:10, 19 ☐
　　15:1, 7 ☐
　　16:1 ☐
　　19:15 ☐

5.   His love and grace

1 John 4:8 & 16 state that God is love, and show that love characterises God's basic approach to people. 1 John 3:1 sets God's love firmly in the context of his fatherhood.

Love, by definition, cannot exist in abstract; it must have an object. The New Testament clearly reveals that people are the objects of God's love, and that – within the Godhead – the Son is the object of the Father's love. We see this, for example, in John 3:16, 35; 5:20; 10:17; 14:21–23; 15:9; 16:27; 17:23.

The New Testament also teaches that God's love:

- *has been poured into our hearts through the Spirit* – Romans 5:5

- *is his saving work for sinners* – Romans 5:8

- *never departs from believers* – Romans 8:39

- *turns believers into conquerors* – Romans 8:37

- *should be the desired aim of our minds* – 2 Thessalonians 3:5

- *is the distinguishing characteristic of the Father* – 2 Corinthians 13:11, 14; Ephesians 6:23

God's grace and mercy are closely linked with his love. We examine the concept of grace in *Salvation by Grace* in this series, but we need to appreciate here that 'the grace of God' is an essential aspect of his fatherly love. The Father's grace means that he gives undeserved favours to the objects of his love, to his children.

We see God's unceasing grace in passages like Romans 3:24; 11:6; 1 Corinthians 1:4; 3:10; 15:10; 2 Corinthians 9:14; Galatians 2:21; Ephesians 1:6; 2:5–7; 2 Timothy 1:9; Titus 2:11; Hebrews 4:16; James 4:6; 1 Peter 4:10 & 5:10–12.

God's mercy is linked to his grace, his love and his righteousness. If the righteous God must condemn whatever is unrighteous, he also must extend mercy to those who should be condemned – because mercy is just as much a part of his nature as righteousness.

Luke 6:36 and 2 Corinthians 1:3 demonstrate that the Father is essentially merciful – this merely reflects Old Testament passages like Exodus 34:6; Psalm 86:15 & 145:8.

1 John 4:8, 16 ☐
3:1 ☐
John 3:16, 35 ☐
5:20 ☐
10:17 ☐
14:21–23 ☐
15:9 ☐
16:27 ☐
17:23 ☐
Romans 5:5 ☐
5:8 ☐
8:37–39 ☐
2 Thessalonians 3:5 ☐
2 Corinthians 13:11–14 ☐
Ephesians 6:23 ☐
Romans 3:24 ☐
11:6 ☐
1 Corinthians 1:4 ☐
3:10 ☐
15:10 ☐
2 Corinthians 9:14 ☐
Galatians 2:21 ☐
Ephesians 1:6 ☐
2:5–7 ☐
2 Timothy 1:9 ☐
Titus 2:11 ☐
Hebrews 4:16 ☐
James 4:6 ☐
1 Peter 4:10 ☐
5:10–12 ☐
Luke 6:36 ☐
2 Corinthians 1:3 ☐
Exodus 34:6 ☐
Psalm 86:15 ☐
145:8 ☐

We see God's mercy in, for example, Luke 18:13; Romans 9:15–18; 11:30–32; 1 Corinthians 7:25; 2 Corinthians 4:1; 1 Timothy 1:16; 1 Peter 2:10 and James 5:11.

6.   His faithfulness and peace

We consider the faith of God in some detail in *Living Faith*. 1 Corinthians 1:9 sets God's faithfulness in the context of his fatherhood, and the wider New Testament teaching shows that God is faithful:

- *in calling people into fellowship with his Son* – 1 Corinthians 1:9

- *in guarding his children against excessive testing of their faith* – 1 Corinthians 10:13

- *in keeping his word* – 2 Corinthians 1:18

- *in protecting them from the evil one* – 2 Thessalonians 3:3

- *to inspire and strengthen suffering believers* – 1 Peter 4:19

- *to forgive sins* – 1 John 1:9

- *even when people are faithless* – 2 Timothy 2:13

Throughout the New Testament, it is constantly assumed that the unceasing and unchanging nature of God means the Father can be trusted to fulfil his promises.

Everything that God gives to his children is an integral part of his nature. He cannot give us anything which is not part of himself. It requires some deep thought to grasp this truth; but it is a foundational truth of Christianity, and has many important applications which we consider throughout this *Sword of the Spirit* series.

All Paul's epistles begin with a blessing which includes 'peace from God'. If peace is a quality that God imparts, it must be an attribute which he possesses. We see this in, for example, Romans 15:33; 1 Corinthians 14:33; Philippians 4:7–9; 1 Thessalonians 5:23.

The presence of peace presupposes the absence of conflict. There is no tension or worry within God. He is never uncertain about his actions or frustrated in his plans. His mind always maintains a perfect equilibrium. At the heart of the universe, behind all the chaos of human affairs, is the God of peace. And it is this personal divine peace which the Father graciously offers to his children.

GOD THE FATHER

Because God is eternal and infinite, no human understanding of him can ever be complete. No summary of biblical passages, no list of names and attributes, can ever present the *full* picture. There must always be a significant element of mystery.

The New Testament suggests, however, that we can know what we need to know about God. This is a basic biblical assumption.

We have established that the Father of the New Testament is the *Yahweh Elohim* of the Old Testament. The Creator of heaven and earth is both fatherly and sovereign; the king of the universe never acts tyrannically because he is a Father; and the righteous judge always acts mercifully because he is shaped by his fatherhood.

We have seen that the Father God is filled with paradoxical attributes, with attributes which seem to be opposites, but which are – in reality – perfectly balanced. His love and wrath, his goodness and righteousness, his mercy and judgement, his transcendence and immanence, and so on, are all presented equally in the New Testament.

Our understanding of God has to be inaccurate if any of the paradoxical aspects of his character are over-looked, over-emphasised, or not held in balance with each other.

The whole of our Christian faith hangs on our knowledge of God; and the whole purpose of our faith is that we might know God – accurately, intimately and personally.

It is simply not possible, for example, to understand the incarnation – the very person of Christ – if we have a wrong idea about God. People who think that God is an angry, remote being who needs to be placated are bound to misunderstand Jesus' mission and ministry. It is only a Father who loves his children who acts to redeem them.

This is why we are considering *Knowing the Father* in this series before *Salvation by Grace*. This book, though perhaps the hardest to study and the most difficult to grasp, is foundational to the entire series. If we do not know the Father, the Son has died in vain.

PART FOUR

the father and the son

In Part One, we saw that the supreme nature of God means there can be only one God. If he is infinite, he both fills everything and is beyond everything. His omnipotence, transcendence and immanence precludes the possibility of there being another similar deity.

In Part Two, however, we noted the Old Testament suggestion that there is some form of plurality within God's nature. It hints that he is 'one, but more-than-one'.

We saw that *Elohim* is a plural noun which takes a singular verb. Genesis 1:26–27, for example, passes backwards and forwards between 'I' and 'we', and 'he' and 'they'. Many scholars insist that *Elohim* is just a common noun, and that its plural form merely conveys the general concept of majestic deity. Yet it is often used as a proper noun, and this suggests that there is something of the corporate about God.

Genesis 1:26–27 ☐

And we observed that God's most common 'trunk' name, *Yahweh Sabaoth*, is usually translated as 'the LORD of Hosts' – meaning 'the Lord who possesses Hosts or Armies'. This can, however, be translated as 'the LORD who is Hosts'; in this case, the divine name *Yahweh Sabaoth* implies that God is not alone.

Genesis 16:7–14 ☐
18:1–33 ☐
22:11–18 ☐
31:11–13 ☐
Exodus 3:1–6 ☐
Judges 2:1–5 ☐
Exodus 33:2–3 ☐

Then there are several Old Testament references to the 'Angel of the LORD' who sometimes appears in human form. This enigmatic being is often recognised as God – as in, for example, Genesis 16:7–14; 18:1–33; 22:11–18; 31:11–13; Exodus 3:1–6 and Judges 2:1–5; yet he is also clearly distinct from God, as in Exodus 33:2–3.

These particular angelic visitations are often considered to be pre-incarnation appearances of Christ, and are usually called either 'theophanies' or 'Christophanies'. The angel is identifiable as God, yet distinguishable from God; and he underlines God's mysterious 'one, but more-than-one' nature.

THE TRIUNE GOD

The New Testament develops the understanding that God is 'one, yet more-than-one', without ever defining him in terms of a Holy Trinity.

The New Testament simply presents information which suggests that Jesus and the Spirit have a divine nature – and that they are one with each other and with God – without drawing any conclusions from this.

There are four groups of passages in the New Testament which imply that God's nature is essentially 'triune' or 'three-in-one'.

1.   Those which use a trinitarian formula

Matthew 28:19 ☐

- Matthew 28:19 links the Name of the Father, the Son and the Spirit together in a 'trinitarian' baptismal formula.

2 Corinthians
13:14 ☐

- 2 Corinthians 13:14 offers a benediction which involves God, the Lord Jesus Christ and the Holy Spirit. No distinction is made between them, and they are clearly presented as 'co-equal'.

Revelation 1:4–8 ☐

- Revelation 1:4–8 refers to God as the one 'who is and was and is to come', to the Spirit as the 'seven-fold Spirit', and to the Son as 'Jesus Christ'.

   The whole of Revelation 1 shows that we can distinguish between the Father, the Son and the Spirit, but that they are all the eternal, majestic, sovereign Almighty.

2.   Those which use a three-fold structure

A second group of passages present God in a distinct triadic, or three-fold, form. For example:

- Ephesians 4:4–6 speaks of 'One Spirit ... one Lord ... one God.

- 1 Corinthians 12:3–6 introduces 'the same Spirit ... the same Lord ... the same God.

- 1 Peter 1:2 uses a triadic structure to stress different functions of the Father, the Spirit and Jesus with, it seems, some sort of sequential link.

- Ephesians 1:3–14 employs the same three-fold sequential struc-ture to point to different divine functions – in verses 3, 5 & 13.

3.   Those which mention the three persons together

Then there are several passages where the Father, the Son and the Spirit are associated without any clear structure.

For example, Mark 1:9–11; Luke 10:21; Romans 8; Galatians 4:4–6; 2 Thessalonians 2:13–14; Titus 3:4–6 and Jude 1:20–21 all link the three persons in a way which does not appear to be accidental.

4.   Those which reveal trinitarian relationships

The link between the Father, the Son and the Spirit is clearest in Jesus' last supper teaching. John 14:16–17, 25–26; 15:26 and 16:13–15 reveal both the relationship and the distinctiveness of the three divine persons.

We see that the Father sends the Spirit in the name of the Son; that the Son sends the Spirit who issues from the Father; and that all three are involved in the revelation of truth to men and women.

A trinitarian relationship can also be seen in passages like John 1:3; Colossians 1:15–17; Hebrews 1:2, which ascribe actions to Jesus that are normally attributed to God.

Tri-unity

As well as pointing to three distinct persons, the New Testament also emphasises the absolute unity or oneness of God. John 10:30 is the

Ephesians 4:4–6 ☐

1 Corinthians 12:3–6 ☐

1 Peter 1:2 ☐

Ephesians 1:3–14 ☐

Mark 1:9–11 ☐

Luke 10:21 ☐

Romans 8 ☐

Galatians 4:4–6 ☐

2 Thessalonians 2:13–14 ☐

Titus 3:4–6 ☐

Jude 1:20–21 ☐

John 14:16–17 ☐
14:25–26 ☐
15:26 ☐
16:13–15 ☐

John 1:3 ☐

Colossians 1:15–17 ☐

Hebrews 1:2 ☐

John 10:30 ☐

John 1:1 ☐
8:24, 28 ☐
10:38 ☐
14:9–11 ☐
17:21–23 ☐

strongest statement, and Jesus' claim that 'the Father and I are one' prompted the Jews to fetch stones to kill him for blasphemy.

John 1:1; 8:24, 28; 10:38; 14:9–11 & 17:21–23 highlight the absolute oneness of the Father and the Son. Like so much about God, this is a mystery which the Bible repeatedly records, but never explains.

We can say that the New Testament develops the Old Testament understanding of God as 'one, but more-than-one' by clarifying the 'more-than-one' element without weakening the stress that he is 'only one'. It reveals that 'more-than-one' really means 'three'; and, therefore, some believers assume that there are *three distinctive beings within God* who, in some mysterious way, are united.

The biblical stress, however, is different, for the New Testament emphasises that *God is one being* whose essence exists eternally in three 'uni-persons'. (As, in recent years, the word 'person' has become increasingly associated with the idea of separate individuals, it is probably better to refer to 'uni-persons' rather than 'persons'.)

It is vital that we grasp this point. The Father, the Son and the Spirit are three self-distinctions within one being, and not three distinct individuals. God is one, he is not divided into three; but he reveals his nature and his oneness in a three-fold diversity of uni-persons, characteristics and functions.

The first person

In this *Sword of the Spirit* series, we focus on the second and third persons of God in separate books – in *Knowing the Son* and in *Knowing the Spirit*. In this book, however, we are considering two related topics: thus far, we have been learning that fatherhood is central to the full nature of the one God; now we are moving on to learn more about the self-distinction within God who is identified as 'the Father'.

We know that, in the Old Testament, the English word *God* always means the 'one, but-more-than-one' God. In the New Testament, however, the word *God* is used to refer both to 'the one God' and to 'the first person of God': this is particularly true in Paul's letters, in Romans – Philemon, where God generally means 'the Father'.

It is usually obvious from the context whether a New Testament reference to *God* means the triune God or the first person of God. In casual reading, however, it is easy to misunderstand a passage – and so overlook the supreme significance of knowing the Father.

Paradoxes

We have seen that every element of God's name and fatherhood must be fully true about the Father, *and* the Son *and* the Spirit. And we have seen that paradoxes like goodness and righteousness, transcendence and immanence, love and wrath, must co-exist within an eternal being.

We should also realise that another group of paradoxes – fatherhood and sonship, leadership and servanthood, will and obedience, glory and humility, self-sufficiency and dependence – must also co-exist within one eternal-and-infinite being. And it is this group of paradoxical aspects which are most clearly visible in the relationship which exists within God between the Father and the Son.

THE FATHER AND THE SON

Matthew 11:25–30, and its parallel passage of Luke 10:21–22, records some of Jesus' most illuminating words about the Father, and about his relationship with the Father.

Luke 10:21 makes it clear that Jesus' words about the Father were Spirit-inspired praise and prayer. It is no different today. We can only know the Father with the help of the Holy Spirit. If we try to know him only by intellectual effort we will end up with an abstract being who is no more than a bundle of words which each begin with 'omni'.

Matthew 11:25 declares that the Father hides his revelation from the 'wise and prudent'. This means that knowledge of the Father can be grasped only as it is given, or revealed, by the Spirit; that we increase our knowledge of the Father by fellowshipping more closely with the Spirit; and that 'babes' are especially qualified to know him because they are not too sophisticated to praise him.

Ephesians 5:19–20 develops this by showing that to be filled with the Spirit is to give praise and thanks to the Father. Quite simply, any

Matthew
11:25–30 ☐

Luke 10:21–22 ☐

Ephesians
5:19–20 ☐

knowledge of God which is not based around Spirit-inspired praise *cannot* include the secrets which the Father shares with the Son in the Spirit.

Mutual dependence

Matthew 11:25–30 & Luke 10:21–22 stress the dependence of the Son on the Father. The Son is not the primary source or possessor of what he reveals to his disciples. It must first be handed to him by his Father.

The Father is first and the Son is second, and the second must receive from the first. Moreover, knowledge of the Son is the right of the Father – which means that the Son depends on the revealing activity of the Father, as John 6:44 underlines.

John 6:44 ☐

This dependence is a major theme of John's Gospel, which constantly stresses that the Son's words, deeds and directions must be received from the Father. We see this, for example, in John 5:19, 30; 6:38; 7:28–29; 8:26, 28–29; 10:18 & 12:49–50.

John 5:19, 30 ☐
6:38 ☐
7:28–29 ☐
8:26 ☐
8:28–29 ☐
10:18 ☐
12:49–50 ☐

The Father, however, also depends on the Son – the first on the second. The Father has committed everything to the Son, and does not act, or speak, or give himself to be known apart from the Son. This does not means that the Father has lost the initiatory control of revelation, because the Son looks to him at every point. Instead, Matthew 11:27 shows that the Father exercises his sovereignty in communion with the Son, who enacts and reveals the Father's will among men and women.

Unique relationship

The relationship between the Father and the Son is at the heart of the gospel, for fatherhood and sonship imply both mutual dependence *and* shared life.

Matthew 11:25–30 & Luke 10:21–22 show that the first and second persons of God share a mutual knowledge which is exclusive to them, and which is opened to men and women only by the will and choice of the Father and the Son.

The unique relationship of the Father and Son is an essential part of the way we know God and what we know about God. To know God is to know the Father through the Son, and the Son through the Father.

As we see in *Knowing the Son*, Jesus is not just 'the' prophet who speaks of and points to a truth which could be revealed by a different prophet; and he is not just 'the' minister of God's truth, for he is himself an essential part of its content. To know God is to know the relationship between the Father in heaven and the Son on earth.

This is particularly clear in Matthew 11:28–30. Many people can tell people to go to God, but only Jesus can urge people to come to him – for to come to him is to come to God.

We can say that the Father is the Lord of heaven and earth, and that the Son is meek and lowly. But in the middle of Jesus' humility and humanity we can always see and hear the divine authority that he shares with the Father. And at the heart of the Father's holy authority we can always find the grace and mercy that he shares with the Son.

We need to grasp that *revelation* and *salvation* are both effected within this unique relationship between the Father and the Son, because their Father/Son relationship constitutes the very life of God.

This means that we do not know revelation or salvation unless we know the Father/Son relationship of God – for both revelation and salvation are divinely intended to draw us into sonship so that we can know the Father.

THE FATHER'S IDENTITY

We have noted the New Testament teaching that it is God's nature and will for the Father to speak and act through his Son. This means that the Father expresses his identity in and through the Son.

John 1:18 reveals two truths:

John 1:18 ☐

1. *the Father expresses his identity in the Son because it is the Son who has made him known*

2. *the Son is identical with the Father in being and nature*

The first of these truths must depend on the second, because only God can perfectly reveal God. Jesus must share the Father's divine nature and being if he is to be an adequate and accurate revelation of the Father. We consider this more fully in *Knowing the Son*.

John 5:17 ☐
14:10–11 ☐

This means that the words and works of Jesus express not only his person and nature, but also the person and nature of the Father.

Jesus constantly claims that his words are the words of God, and that his deeds are the deeds of God – because his being is identical with the being of God. We see this in passages like John 5:17 and 14:10–11.

In *Living Faith*, we see that, for us, confessing God's Word and doing God's Word are inseparable, and that, for God, revelation and salvation are twin aspects of his faith. The demonstration of the union between Father and Son *is* the mighty works and words of Jesus – in which he and the Father are both involved in their different ways.

It is important that we understand this truth. The God of the New Testament is not an abstract bundle of 'omnis' who allows us a glimpse into his eternal nature through Jesus.

Instead, he is the God who intervenes; he is the 'Transcendental Interferer' who comes and changes things; he is the heavenly Father who speaks and acts, who loves and deals in saving grace, who protects and provides for his creatures and children, who counts the hairs on our heads and feels pain when even a sparrow falls to the ground.

God makes himself known as the Father who makes the blind see, the deaf hear, the lame walk, the dead rise. He is the Father who works salvation – and whose words and works are known and effected through his Son.

The simple truth is that there is no word or work of the Son which is not also a word and work of the Father.

THE FATHER'S PARTNERSHIP

It is a fundamental New Testament assumption that Jesus is the essential partner of the Father in all God's dealings with humanity. We can say that the coming, living, dying, rising Jesus is the indispensable clue to the Father's purpose in *creation*, *redemption* and *judgement*.

While it is true that we cannot know the Father except by knowing the Son, we must not forget that we know the Son *so that* we can know the Father. Many believers need an occasional reminder that the Father is the primary focus of the Christian faith, and not the Son or the Spirit.

1.   partners in creation

John 1:3; Colossians 1:15–17 and Hebrews 1:2 show that the Father works through the Son in creation.

John 1:3 ☐

Colossians
            1:15–17 ☐

Hebrews 1:2 ☐

Jesus is the agent and the final purpose of all creation, and we should not think or speak about God's work in creation without appreciating the Father/Son relationship which established and sustains it. In fact, we can say that the Father's action in Christ is before, behind, underneath, over, in, around and beyond everything to do with our natural universe.

2.   partners in redemption

It is the same in salvation: the Father does not act without the Son. Our restored relationship with the Father depends entirely on the life, death and resurrection of the Son.

Passages like John 3:16 and 2 Corinthians 5:18–19 shows how the Father's saving action moves from the one to many, from its centre in Christ to all humanity.

John 3:16 ☐

2 Corinthians
            5:18–19 ☐

It is not enough for our understanding and celebration of redemption to focus only on Jesus – we must appreciate that salvation depends on the Father working in and through the Son.

As we see in *Salvation by Grace*, the full process of redemption involves being saved:

- *from sin*

- *by grace*

- *through faith in Jesus*

- *into fellowship with the Father in the Spirit*

Many believers rejoice in the first three elements of salvation, but fail to realise that the purpose of redemption is that they might know the Father, and live in fellowship with him in the sort of mutual dependence that we see between the Father and the Son.

John 3:18 ☐

5:22 ☐

Acts 17:31 ☐

Ephesians 1:10 ☐

Philippians
2:9–11 ☐

1 Corinthians
15:28 ☐

3.   partners in judgement

It is the same at the last day. The Father may be the source of God's judgement, but it is the Son who executes his judgement – we see this throughout Revelation, and in John 3:18; 5:22 and Acts 17:31.

We also see the Father and Son at work at the last day in the completion of the kingdom and the new heaven and earth. Ephesians 1:10; Philippians 2:9–11 and 1 Corinthians 15:28 show that the focus is on Jesus, but that the priority of the Father is paramount.

God the Father

We have seen that the Father always speaks and works through his Son – from creation, through the incarnation, to the final judgement.

Every aspect of God's name and nature, every element of his eternal fatherhood, is seen and heard in the Father/Son relationship which was revealed 2,000 years ago and is recorded now in the New Testament.

This means that we must move beyond thinking about God in abstract terms, and begin to appreciate what the Father speaking and acting through the Son really means. We can say, for example, that:

- *the love of God* is not a perfect ideal of love; it is the practical love which, in the grace of the Son, comes to seek and to save those who are separated from the Father, and to establish for them – at enormous divine cost – eternal fellowship with the Father.

- *the power of God* is not a generalised sovereign omnipotence, it is the specific power by which the infinite spiritual Son revealed the infinite spiritual Father by becoming a finite material human, and by healing the sick, enduring the cross and rising from the dead.

- *the truth of God* is not an ethical or philosophical body of ideas, it is the personal words and thoughts of the Father which are expressed in the person, the words and the actions of the Son.

Matthew 11:27 ☐

To think like this about God – in a practical, relational way – is merely to apply the truth of Matthew 11:27 that we have already considered. It is to recognise that the Father has delivered all things to the Son, and that no one knows the Father except the Son – and those men and women to whom the Son chooses to reveal him. We should never stop thanking God that we are among those people.

PART FIVE

the father and the spirit

We began Part Four by examining God's triune nature, and then moved on to consider the biblical teaching about 'the Father and the Son'. In this chapter, we are building on exactly the same examination of God's triune nature in our study of 'the Father and the Spirit'.

The New Testament introduces the Holy Spirit as the third member of the Trinity, and makes it plain that he is fully personal *and* fully divine. If 'the Spirit' was merely a metaphor for God's power, the New Testament would not continually name the Spirit as 'him' rather than 'it', and it would not show him acting in a thoroughly personal manner.

For example, the New Testament reveals that the Spirit hears, helps, witnesses, convinces, convicts, commands, declares, leads, guides, grieves, teaches, forbids, opposes, desires, speaks and gives speech.

Of course, it could be argued that grieving the Spirit simply means grieving God. But it is unlikely that he could do *all* these things if he were not a distinct person. The Spirit, however, also intercedes with the Father, and it would be impossible for him to do this if he were merely an extension of God. So it is the Spirit's special ministry of intercession which proves his distinctive personhood.

Furthermore, if 'the Holy Spirit' was simply just another way of describing God's presence, the New Testament would not make it so clear that he is God, yet is distinct from 'the Father' and 'the Son'.

Passages like Matthew 28:19; Acts 5:3–4; 1 Corinthians 12:4–6; 2 Corinthians 13:14; Ephesians 1:3–14; 2:18; 3:14–19; 4:4–6; 2 Thessalonians 2:13–14; 1 Peter 1:2; & Revelation 1:4–5 link the Father, the Son and the Spirit together in a way which shows that the Spirit really is Almighty God.

John 14:26; 15:26; 16:8 and 16:13–14 point particularly clearly to the distinct personhood of the Spirit. These verses contain the emphatic pronoun *ekeinos* ('he') in the masculine, when the noun *pneuma* ('Spirit') is neuter in Greek and the corresponding word in Aramaic (the language Jesus spoke) is feminine.

Although this device is lost in English translations, it is conspicuous in Greek and shows that the Spirit is a 'he' and not an 'it'.

This use of *ekeinos* is especially striking because the grammatically correct neuter pronouns are used in John 14:17, when the Spirit is first introduced. This demonstrates that the switch to the masculine in verse 26 is not a mistake; it is a pointer to the personality of the Spirit.

Jesus and the apostles clearly recognised that the person of the Spirit was active in the Old Testament, and that Old Testament passages about God's breath referred to the Spirit's personal activity. For example:

- *Mark 12:36, Acts 1:16 & 4:25* – David is said to have spoken by the Holy Spirit in 2 Samuel 23:2

- *Luke 4:18–21* – Jesus, filled with the power of the personal Holy Spirit, claims that his preaching fulfils Isaiah's witness to his own anointing by the Spirit in Isaiah 61:1–4

- *John 3:5–10* – Jesus rebukes Nicodemus for not realising that his teaching on the new birth of 'water and the Spirit' looks back to Ezekiel 36:25–27 & 37:1–14

- *Acts 28:25; Hebrews 3:7 & 10:15–17* – Old Testament teaching with a New Testament application is ascribed to the Spirit

- *Acts 2:16–18* – Peter identifies the outpouring of the personal Spirit as that predicted in Joel 2:28–29

We examine the total ministry of the Spirit in *Knowing the Spirit* and we consider our partnership with the Spirit in *Ministry in the Spirit*. In this book, however, we study how the Spirit's ministry relates to the fatherhood of God.

The New Testament mentions two declarations which are the result of the Spirit's work in the lives of believers:

- *Jesus is Lord* – 1 Corinthians 12:3

- *Abba, Father* – Romans 8:15 & Galatians 4:6

As we see in *Knowing the Spirit*, these twin phrases describe and define the essential ministry of the Spirit in the world and in the church.

We become members of Christ's body by our relationship to, and our confession of, the Son and the Father. And it is the Spirit's work both to create the relationship and to inspire the confession. Quite simply, the two most fundamental questions for every believer to answer are:

- *am I living under the lordship of Jesus?*

- *do I know God as Father?*

We examine the work of the Spirit in relation to the lordship of Jesus in *The Rule of God*. Here, however, we focus on the Spirit's work in helping us to know the Father.

ABBA

It is, perhaps, not strictly accurate to classify 'Abba, Father' as a declaration of precisely the same type as 'Jesus is Lord'.

The phrase, 'Jesus is Lord', is clearly *a confession of faith* which is directed towards the people around us, and should be the foundation of all Christian living and witnessing.

But the phrase, 'Abba, Father', is more *a cry of praise* which is directed at God, and should be the basis of all Christian praying and praising. As we see in *Knowing the Spirit*, the Holy Spirit seeks to inspire and empower both *our witness* and *our worship*.

1 Corinthians 12:3 ☐

Romans 8:15 ☐

Galatians 4:6 ☐

The cry of praise, 'Abba Father', does not primarily describe God (though it does do that), rather, it essentially describes the way that we approach God as Father, in the access that the Spirit provides.

A trinitarian cry

We should be able to appreciate that the 'Abba' cry of praise is thoroughly trinitarian in its context and meaning.

The very word 'Abba' itself makes it clear that the new name we use to address God is not one which we have chosen or invented. It comes from Jesus, who first spoke to God in this way.

Whenever we approach God crying 'Abba', we are implicitly acknowledging that we have learnt this way of approach from the Son. Our right to address God as 'Abba' comes from the Son, and is given to us by the Spirit – who takes what was first in Christ and makes it real for us.

Quite simply, we approach the Father and call him 'Abba' through the Son and in the Spirit.

THE BACKGROUND OF ABBA

Christian people in every age and tradition, of every nation and language, have used the word 'Abba' in their particular culture and context. To understand it accurately, however, we need to appreciate its meaning in the particular culture and context in which the Father chose to reveal himself as 'Abba' through the Son.

There are two aspects to this, and we need to appreciate them both equally.

1. The Jewish background

In Jesus' day, the idea of fatherhood was quite different from ours today. In the story of the prodigal son, for example, it is clearly assumed that a son will exist in lifelong dependence on his father.

THE FATHER AND THE SPIRIT

Luke 15:11–32 describes the elder son doing what was expected of sons in that culture – he stayed near the father, worked under his direction, depended on his provision and remained under his authority. Luke 15:11–32 ☐

The younger son sinned against the father, not only by his unhealthy lifestyle, but also by seeking independence and leaving the father's home. For us today, however, it is a sign of maturity when an adult son leaves his father's home and lives independently.

In Jesus' day, every father was the absolute provider and sovereign protector of all his children, for all his life. We have moved away from this first century patriarchal approach, but we still need to recognise the cultural background in which God's fatherhood was revealed.

In the New Testament, the first person of God is not a twentieth century father; he is a first century father who has authoritative and absolute rights over even his adult sons and daughters. He expects all his children to stay close to him, to depend on him, to honour him, to obey him, to reveal the family name and nature – and to provide him with many 'grandchildren'.

When the Spirit leads us to the Father, when he seeks to deepen our relationship with the Father, when he inspires us to cry 'Abba', he is pointing us to our absolute provider and sovereign protector – and not to an indulgent, absent, unreliable daddy.

2.   The religious background

We have noted that 'Abba' was first spoken among Jews who already knew that 'father' was a basic name or title of God. The very fact that 'Abba' is an Aramaic word rather than a Greek word suggests that we need to understand it in an Old Testament context.

The Old Testament often describes fathers as loving their sons, but it suggests that sons respond to their fathers with honour and respect rather than affection. This is true both of human fathers, as in Exodus 20:12, and of God, as in Jeremiah 31:18–20. In this passage, God's yearning for Ephraim is compared to the compassion of a father for a lost son. But the son does not say 'Abba, Father' on his return – only the more formal and reverent, 'You are *Yahweh*, my *Elohim*'. Exodus 20:12 ☐ Jeremiah 31:18–20 ☐

In the Old Testament, God is addressed as 'Father' only in the context of looking forward prophetically to Israel's final salvation.

Isaiah 63:7–16 ☐

We note the significance of Isaiah 63:7–16 in *Knowing the Spirit*: but not only does this remarkable trinitarian passage identify the Spirit of *Yahweh* as 'Holy Spirit', it also identifies *Yahweh* as 'Our Father' and as the 'Saviour'. The triune insights we gained in Part Four help us to understand this passage more deeply.

It is vital that we appreciate the importance of this point. In the Old Testament, with all its rich understanding of God's name and nature, it is only when a Spirit-anointed and Spirit-inspired prophet looks forward to God's redeeming activity that he suddenly recognises *Yahweh* as 'Our Father, our Redeemer'. Quite simply, we cannot know the Father without the help of the Holy Spirit.

Psalm 89:19–26 ☐

We also see this principle in Psalm 89:19–26. This is a prophetic Psalm which looks forward to the messianic king. He is the one whom will be anointed by God with divine holy oil – with the Spirit – and he is the one who will cry, 'Your are my Father, my *Elohim*, and the rock of my salvation'.

This means that the religious background to knowing God as 'Abba' is not the context of a benevolent creator who cares for his children; it is the context of a coming Spirit-anointed Redeemer.

Jesus' use of 'Abba' points directly to Isaiah 63 and Psalm 89, and shows the supreme importance of knowing the Father as Redeemer through the Spirit.

GETHSEMANE

Mark 14:35–36 ☐

It is impossible to overstate the importance of the context in which the Scriptures record Jesus addressing God as 'Abba'. In the light of the Old Testament redemptive background, we should not be surprised to find 'Abba' on the lips of Jesus in the garden of Gethsemane as he waits for Judas in the shadow of the cross. We read this in Mark 14:35–36.

This suggests that to be a child of the Father, to approach him as 'Abba', involves a willingness to accept his will – even to the extent of accepting the suffering and sacrifice of the cross.

Jesus' cry of 'Abba' in Gethsemane underlines that 'the Father' is both the stern first century Jewish patriarch who must be unflinchingly obeyed throughout his children's lives, and also the anointed Redeemer whose greatest passion is to accomplish his children's salvation.

We develop this in Parts Six and Seven by considering 'the Father and the cross' and 'the Father's will' in more detail – before moving on in Part Eight to 'worship the Father' with the cries of praise that the Spirit inspires.

Gethsemane shows that the unique relationship of the Son to the Father does not exempt the Son from the obedience which is inherent in the Father-Son relationship. On the contrary, the Son's unique relationship demands the unique obedience of the cross.

All this means that whenever the Spirit inspires us to cry 'Abba', he is inspiring us to remember the cross and to obey the Father in a similar sacrificial way.

The redeeming Father

Jesus' Gethsemane use of 'Abba' proves that God's eternal divine fatherhood is nothing like twentieth century human fatherhood, so – as we have already noted – we should not think about God in the image of our own human fathers.

Instead, we should think about him in terms of Gethsemane, as the Son composes himself to execute the Father's work of redemption. We cannot understand or use 'Abba' correctly in any other way.

This suggests that we should not think about 'the Father' within a generalised concept of fatherhood, but rather within the specific concept of the redemptive death and resurrection of the Son – as it is revealed by the Spirit.

Put simply, the Father is known through the Son and revealed by the Spirit. This means we can say that:

- *God is 'Abba' because he wills the obedience of the cross to achieve his redemptive purpose for his children.*

- *God is first known as 'Abba' by Jesus, and his 'abbahood' becomes widely known only as Jesus draws people to 'Abba' through the Spirit.*

- *God has not always been the 'Abba' of everybody; instead, Jesus announces the gospel that God is his Father and that he wants to be ours too – as we are drawn by the Spirit into the fellowship of faith and obedience which Jesus shows in Gethsemane.*

- *The 'Our Father' is not the prayer of all people everywhere, it is the prayer of disciples who are following the one who cried 'Abba' in Gethsemane.*

THE ACTIVITY OF THE SPIRIT

It is not enough for us to understand the background of 'Abba' and to grasp its redemptive significance in Gethsemane, we also need to cry it in praise – and this is the work of the Holy Spirit.

God's fatherhood must not be central only to our *understanding* of God, it must also be central to our *experience* of him. We should remember that we are called to know the Father relationally, and not merely to know him propositionally.

Furthermore, a Christian believer is not just a person who has been regenerated by the Spirit and converted to Christ – he is also a child who cries 'Abba' to the Father.

But nothing in our life of faith is automatic. In theory, conversion to Christ, anointing with the Spirit, and fellowship with the Father are inseparable aspects of God's salvation – for the biblical Jesus is the way to the Father and the baptiser in the Spirit.

In reality, however, there are many believers who trust in Christ but do not know the Spirit's power or have much confidence in the Father.

There can be few Christians who do not believe in the fatherhood of God, but not all believers enter into the intimate, personal relationship with the Father which is open to them. We do this only as a result of the ministry of the Holy Spirit, as God sends the Spirit of his Son into our lives crying 'Abba, Father'.

Sons and daughters

It should be obvious that knowing God's fatherhood implies knowing our status as sons and daughters. The Spirit who cries 'Abba Father' in Romans 8:15 is the Spirit who witnesses to our spirits that we are children of God.

Romans 8:15 ☐

This means that knowledge of the Father is knowledge of ourselves. We learn who we are by discovering our relationship to God. The fact that, in Christ, God has made himself our Father and us his children is surely the most significant and therapeutic fact that we can learn.

This discovery is a free gift of the Spirit, for he makes real within us what Christ has achieved on our behalf. This is very clear in Romans 8:16 and Galatians 4:6: the cry is not spoken by us, it is the Spirit's cry to us and through us. This means that we need to hear the Spirit saying 'Abba' in our spirits before we can speak it ourselves.

Romans 8:16 ☐

Galatians 4:6 ☐

We have seen that Jesus found the strength and obedience for all his words and deeds – including his dying and rising – in his relationship with the Father. And we know that it is the work of the Spirit to take the things of Jesus and make them real to us – so that we participate in them as partners. As we note throughout this *Sword of the Spirit* series, this is the basis of every gift of grace.

It is also, therefore, the basis of the foundation gift of grace: the Spirit seeks to draw us into the Son's relationship with the Father so that we can share in it in some way as a fellowshipper, as a partner.

Deep, deep within us, the Holy Spirit cries to us to convince us that the 'Abba' Father of Jesus is our Father too. It is only as we respond to the Spirit's cries with living faith that we begin to know the Father.

Heirs

Both Romans 8 and Galatians 4 move directly from 'sonship' to 'inheritance', for it is the children who inherit from their parents.

Romans 8:14–30 ☐

Galatians
3:26–4:7 ☐

This inheritance is described throughout Romans 8, but verse 17 is particularly important. The heirs are known by their relationship to their Father – which is the same as that of the principle heir. The family likeness, the divine name and nature which we considered in Part Two, and which is seen most clearly in Jesus, develops in the lives of the Father's true heirs. And this is the work of the Spirit.

True heirs reveal the same self-giving dependence and obedience as the principle heir; the same grace and mercy towards the sinful and needy; the same Gethsemane glory and acceptance; the same holiness, power and authority; the same mixture of paradoxes – dying and rising, serving and reigning, suffering and victory, humility and confidence, weakness and power, transcendent light and immanent salt, and so on.

This is the great challenge of knowing the Father: those who are his redeemed sons and daughters, those who are privileged to share his 'Name', are those who are expected to share his nature – like Jesus in the garden of Gethsemane.

We must recognise that it is as the Son reaffirms his 'Abba' relationship in Gethsemane that he receives the strength to inherit his Easter glory. And it is as we become sure of our 'sonship' that we receive what we need to go on to receive our inheritance.

Romans 8:17 and Galatians 4:7 both stress that being an heir is a direct consequence of being a child. And Romans 8:17 shows that the context within which heirs approach their Father as 'Abba' must always have something of Gethsemane about it.

Gethsemane is the place where the Son finally rests in the security of the Father's love – and knows that he can trust it, and all the provision that it will make for him. But it is also the place where the Son is called to a new and costly obedience, where he realises that the way ahead will involve death and glory.

This is what knowing the Father means, and this is the promised inheritance of all God's children. As we see in *Glory in the Church*, glory is our destiny, but the path to glory is the pavement of sacrifice.

Sanctification

It should be plain that the inheritance of the Father's name and nature involves sanctification. We consider this in Part Six of *Knowing the Spirit*, where we see that this is an important element in the ministry of the Holy Spirit.

The family likeness, that the Spirit wants to develop in us, has at its centre the absolute obedience of the Son to the Father and the mutual dependence of the Son and the Father. As we allow the Spirit to work in us and through us, so we more closely resemble the family Name.

True Christian maturity is not just looking back at the beginning of the Christian life to Jesus on the cross (though it involves that); it is not just looking out at the functioning of the Christian life in the Spirit's power (though it involves that too); true Christian maturity also lies in looking towards the Father, in looking forward with hope to the goal of the Christian life when we are brought to mature completion and are ready to be received by the Father and joined to the Son.

1 Thessalonians 5:23–24 shows that our Father is the God of complete sanctification, of total peace and wholeness. And Matthew 5:48 teaches that it is Jesus' great purpose to draw every believer to our heavenly Father's absolute perfection, to his eternal-and-infinite completion.

1 Thessalonians 5:23–24 ☐

Matthew 5:48 ☐

We see in *The Rule of God* that the reality of the Father's rule transforms our relationships and attitudes. Human rules give way to a personal relationship with the Father who directs us individually by the Spirit, and provides us in the Spirit with all the resources that we need to keep his rule. Eternal peace and wholeness are the inevitable result.

In Acts 1:4, Jesus promises that the Spirit whom the Son will send is 'the promise of the Father'. The promised Spirit has come from the Father to connect us to the Father, and he has been sent by the one who is complete in the Father to make us complete in him too.

Acts 1:4 ☐

As we hear the Holy Spirit crying 'Abba' in our spirits by faith, as we willingly and eagerly partner the Spirit in crying 'Abba, Father' in our lives, so our sanctification develops towards glorious completion in the Father.

PART SIX

the father and the cross

Once again, our examination of God's triune nature at the beginning of Part Four is the basis for our consideration of the Father and the cross in this chapter. For it is the relationship between the Father, the Son and the Spirit – their oneness, distinctiveness and divine paradoxes – which enables us to understand the cross.

The events of the cross clearly reveal the triune nature of God. They manifest the unique relationship between the Son and the Father, and make possible the movement of the Spirit from the Father to us.

The cross is not only central to the Christian faith, it is also at the heart of God: it divides and joins the three persons and reveals them in quite specific ways. For example, the distinction between the Father and the Son is expressed at Calvary in the Father's abandonment of the Son to sin and death; and their divine oneness is seen in the Father's raising of the Son from death and their united sending of the Spirit.

We consider the events and achievements of the cross more completely in *Salvation by Grace*; here, however, we consider them particularly from the Father's perspective to discover what we can learn about him from Calvary.

WHY THE CROSS?

The New Testament teaches that humanity is characterised by rebellion and disobedience – which we can summarise in the simple word, 'No'. All men and women have said 'No' to God's will and God's grace, and have chosen to rule their own lives. God has responded to this human 'No' in the only holy way that he can – with righteous judgement.

Abandonment

Most church leaders rightly emphasise passages like 2 Thessalonians 1:6–11 and teach that the righteous God *judges* and *punishes* human disobedience. Yet we must also recognise the New Testament truth that God's punishment is often expressed in an active *abandonment* to the consequences of sin. We see this aspect of divine punishment, for example, in Romans 1:18–32.

Romans 1:18–28 ☐

Verse 18 teaches that God has revealed his wrath against human wickedness, and verses 24, 26 and 28 then demonstrate that God's wrath is actively expressed in holy abandonment.

- *we are abandoned to the sinful desires of our hearts*

- *we are abandoned to our shameful lusts*

- *we are abandoned to our depraved minds*

The Greek verb *paradidomi* – which is used here three times – means to 'give over', 'hand over', 'deliver' or 'abandon', and shows that God's abandonment is active rather than passive. This verb is also used in Romans 8:32 to describe how the Father deals with human rebellion.

Romans 8:32 ☐

This abandonment is an inevitable consequence of God's absolute holiness. The Father's moral perfection compels him to withdraw from sin; and it is his righteous judgement which allows the forces of sin and death to operate in a more unrestrained way.

Human rebellion and disobedience are essentially a rebellion against life as God intends it, and the judgement of the infinitely loving God is to allow humans to have their own way – until we discover that our rejection of God's life inevitably results in death.

But the Father's love and mercy mean that his abandonment is not absolute. Through the incarnation and the cross, he has acted to rescue those whom he has abandoned to sin's power and its Romans 6:23 price. He has sent his only Son to identify himself with humanity by being treated as one who is himself abandoned and given up by God.

Romans 6:23 ☐

Acceptance

Divine obedient acceptance is the only antidote to human disobedient abandonment – an acceptance which is characterised by a 'Yes' to everything that the Father is, says and does.

Human rebellion can be ended and reversed only by a 'Yes' to God which is spoken from *within the humanity* which is dominated by disobedience and sin. And divine abandonment can be dealt with only by being accepted and received from *within God* himself.

On the cross, Jesus voluntarily positioned himself between human sin and divine wrath – these then focused entirely on him. Human sin climaxed in its attack on God's Son, but was eternally countered by his willing acceptance of God's will and by his forgiving grace. And the Father's punishing abandonment of the Son to death was the total execution and exhaustion of God's wrath at human sin. We see this in 2 Corinthians 5:21 and John 12:31.

2 Corinthians 5:21 ☐

John 12:31 ☐

This means that, in his obedient acceptance, Jesus replaced our 'No' of rebellion with an eager 'Yes' to God's will and grace. He spoke this 'Yes' on our behalf, from within humanity, so that we could be reconciled with God.

He also spoke 'Yes' to God's judgement by accepting it to himself in solidarity with sinful humanity – he abandoned himself to death in willing obedience to the Father. We see this in Mark 14:36.

Mark 14:36 ☐

In offering obedience and bearing judgement on behalf of all humanity, the Son says 'Yes' to the Father. And in raising Jesus from death, the Father says 'Yes' to the Son – and so to all on whose behalf he is acting. In this, in him, lies our salvation.

Many believers are used to focusing on the Son's actions when they think about the cross. But we must not overlook 2 Corinthians 5:18, which shows that redemption is from 'Our Father, our Redeemer' – it is his initiative, his action, and he is the focus of all the activity.

2 Corinthians 5:18 ☐

THE FATHER'S INITIATIVE

When Jesus died on the cross, many people thought that they were responsible. For example:

- *Judas Iscariot* believed that Jesus had died because he had betrayed him to his enemies

- *Caiaphas* assumed that Jesus had died because he had demanded his death

- *Pontius Pilate* thought that Jesus had died because he had sentenced him to death

- *the people* believed that Jesus had died because they had pleaded for Barabbas' release

- *the Roman soldiers* assumed that Jesus had died because they had executed him.

They were all right. They had killed Jesus. But they were also all wrong, because the events of the cross had their primary source in the will and gracious initiative of the Father. It was his plan, his idea, his will, his good purpose.

Many believers concentrate on the Son's voluntary sacrifice when they think about the cross, and ignore the Father's gift of the sacrifice. Others contrast the Son's love in dying with the Father's wrath which needed placating. Both these approaches overlook the essential oneness of God and make it difficult for people to be confident that the Father's love is at the heart of all God's dealings with humanity.

Whenever the Father's gracious initiative in redemption is missed or misunderstood, his fatherly love is inevitably slandered – and we are robbed of a key element of our assurance. Sadly, in many traditions, there are believers who think that they must hide behind the gentle love of Jesus to be saved from the only-just-contained wrath of a still-angry Father. It is hard for them to revel in their wonderful status as sons and daughters of the all-loving Father.

2 Corinthians 5:18–21 makes it plain that God is the gracious initiator of redemption: we also see this in Romans 5:8 and 8:3. In Part Nine of *Living Faith*, we note that Mark 14:27; John 3:16; Romans 3:25;

2 Corinthians
5:18–21 ☐

Romans 5:8 ☐
8:3 ☐

Mark 14:27 ☐

John 3:16 ☐

Romans 3:25 ☐

4:25; 8:3, 32 and 1 John 4:9–10 all stress that *the Father* sent the Son to redeem humanity.

Of course, elsewhere in the New Testament, the voluntary nature of Christ's sacrifice is also stressed: Matthew 20:28; Galatians 2:20; Ephesians 5:2, 25; 1 Timothy 2:6; Titus 2:14 and Hebrews 9:14, 26 affirm that the Son sacrificed himself.

As we now know that the Father and the Son share the same nature, and that the Son expresses the Father's identity in the world, this should no longer surprise us. The Father gave the Son and the Son freely gave himself. The Father did not make the Son endure an ordeal that he was unwilling to bear, and the Son did not surprise the Father by his selfless action. This is yet another divine paradox, and it is neatly stated in Galatians 1:4 and John 10:17–18.

John 3:16 is rightly one of the most famous verses in the Bible, and loudly declares that redemption has its origin in the Father: it was the Father who so loved the world that he gave his Son.

This means we must recognise that the love and grace of the Father are not the result of redemption – they are its origin, its motivation, even its pre-condition. The obedience of the Son in Gethsemane and on the cross is merely a response to the love-filled will of the Father. We need to keep on reminding ourselves about this if we are to appreciate the Father's great love for us and rejoice in his fatherhood.

THE FATHER'S ACTIVITY

If we think of the Father, the Son and the Spirit as separate individuals, we inevitably caricature Calvary as either God punishing an innocent Jesus or as Jesus persuading a reluctant father.

But 2 Corinthians 5:18–19 establishes that our redemption was not achieved by Christ alone – or by the Father alone – but by the Father acting in and through the Son with his full agreement. They worked in harmony. Their wills were one; they would not be separated.

The essential unity of God could lead us to conclude that God died for us: 1 Corinthians 2:8 may even seem to suggest this. But God's

Romans 4:25 ☐
8:3, 32 ☐

1 John 4:9–10 ☐

Matthew 20:28 ☐

Galatians 2:20 ☐

Ephesians 5:2, 25 ☐

1 Timothy 2:6 ☐

Titus 2:14 ☐

Hebrews 9:14, 26 ☐

Galatians 1:4 ☐

John 10:17–18 ☐
3:16 ☐

2 Corinthians
5:18–19 ☐

1 Corinthians 2:8 ☐

Hebrews 2:14–18 ☐

Philippians 2:6–8 ☐

Romans 8:3 ☐

1 John 4:10 ☐

Ephesians 2:1 ☐

2 Corinthians
5:17 ☐

John 3:7 ☐

immortality means that he could not have died. To solve this problem, God became human so that he could die in our place, and could dispense and receive his own judgement. Hebrews 2:14–18 and Philippians 2:6–8 make this clear.

This means that redemption must be the Father's activity, but that *it must be God acting as a human.* The One who obeys the Father on our behalf must be fully human, or else his obedience and suffering are not relevant to us. And he must also be fully divine, or else his acceptance of abandonment would not make a scrap of difference. This is the truth which passages like Romans 8:3 and 1 John 4:10 expound.

There are three reasons why redemption must be the Father's action:

1.   Human incapacity

We know that, because of sin, it is impossible for men and women to accomplish their own redemption – even with the help of the Spirit.

Ephesians 2:1 graphically describes our fallen human nature, and the sort of changes which are outlined in 2 Corinthians 5:17 and John 3:7 are simply beyond the realms of possibility of fallen human effort.

The whole New Testament teaches that there is no human work which can meet God's perfect requirements. This means that redemption must be the Father's activity – and that we can benefit only from what is done for us by the Father through the Son.

The more we recognise our human sinful incapacity, the more we will realise the need for the Father to work redemption through incarnation. Nothing else makes any sort of sense.

2.   Divine grace

We also know that redemption is an act of grace. By definition, this means that redemption must be an action which is performed exclusively and completely by God himself.

We must understand that there can be no grace if the Father sends someone other than himself to accomplish our redemption.

Even a man who is filled with the Spirit to the nth degree is other than God in his essence – his actions could point to a divine attitude but they could not themselves be a divine action.

For redemption to be a work of grace, it simply must be the Father who brings it about. By now, we should be able to recognise that, to be possible, this requires both a triune God and the incarnation.

It is this act of grace which negates the charge of injustice. Some people accuse Christians of celebrating a terrible wrong, of revering the punishment of an innocent man. But God himself provided the sacrifice, and God himself became the sacrifice. Far from being a gross injustice, the cross is a demonstration of infinite grace.

3. Eternal consequences

We also know that the New Testament represents Christ's death as possessing eternal consequences, as being an action on a par with creation and the final judgement. Galatians 4:4–5 and John 12:31–32 show that the events on the cross effect the destiny of the whole universe, and of every person in it.

Galatians 4:4–5 ☐

John 12:31–32 ☐

The cross is not only the supreme revelation of God's glory and nature (though it is that); the cross is also an action which changes everything. On behalf of all men and women, the Father, in-and-through the Son, reconstitutes humanity's relationship with himself.

The cross is eternally effective as the Father's redeeming action for humanity, and it demands a response from all people. The cross has changed humanity's situation in such a total way that everyone must eventually come to terms with it. 2 Corinthians 5:14–21 proves that the cross is the Father's action, and that it has eternal consequences.

2 Corinthians 5:14–21 ☐

Once we accept this great change, we must recognise that only the Father can bring it about. If redemption is as significant as creation and judgement, only the Creator and Judge could achieve it – by becoming human in his Son to be the Saviour and Redeemer of the world.

THE FATHER'S OUTCOME

Many believers seem to think that the cross deals essentially with human sin. But, before this, it must deal with God's wrath. We can say that, on the cross, Jesus deals more with the Father than with us.

On our behalf, he offers the obedient acceptance which fulfils the Father's will and bears the Father's judgement.

Jesus suffers the Father's abandonment, offers the trust and love which correspond exactly with the Father's, commends his work into the Father's hands, and awaits his verdict. The focus is all on the Father – what will he do?

Praise God, we know that the Father accepts the obedient Son who has exhausted his judgement against sin, acknowledges that the Son has done this on our behalf, and then releases the Holy Spirit to work out all the different 'new births' and 'new creations' in us.

John 16:7 ☐   John 16:7 makes it plain that the Son must first go to the Father before the Spirit can come to work out the new situation in us. The Father is the focus of the cross, and the outcome of redemption is entirely his.

Assurance

It should be clear that the Father's acceptance of the Son has considerable implications for our assurance. If our understanding of redemption focuses on our feelings about our forgiveness, our assurance will largely depend on the state of our personal emotions. If we do not feel forgiven, we will wonder whether we really are!

But our confidence in the cross does not depend on our feelings; it depends on the fact that the Father has said 'Yes' to the Son, has raised *him* from the dead, has received *him* into heaven, and has released the Spirit into the church.

This means that our assurance rests not in our subjective feelings about forgiveness, but in the objective fact of the resurrection – which is the Father's 'Yes' to the Son, to his work, and to all those on whose behalf the Son's work was undertaken.

The outcome of the cross is not that it has prompted the Father to love us a little bit more (for he always has loved us with an infinite love); and it is not that it has turned God into a Father (for he has been the Father throughout all eternity); rather, it is that, through the cross, *the* Father has become *my* Father. It is for this that we should give him unceasing praise and thanks.

THE FATHER'S GRIEF

Many preachers dwell at great length on the Son's sufferings at Calvary, and we consider these in *Salvation by Grace* and *Knowing the Son*. There is, however, another side to the relationship, and we should not neglect the sacrifice of the Father in giving up his Son to death.

We have seen that the natures of the Father, the Son and the Spirit are identical, but that their functions are distinct. The Father and the Son, for example, are equally and identically characterised by love and sacrifice, but they are functionally distinct in that the Father wills and the Son executes the will, the Father sends and the Son is sent, the Father gives and the Son is given.

Romans 8:32 focuses on the Father and shows that he surrendered something of himself in the surrender of the Son – the nature is the same but the function is distinct. In his surrender, the Son suffers abandonment and death, whereas the Father who surrenders his Son suffers the infinite grief of love.

Romans 8:32 ☐

If we are to understand this aspect of the cross correctly, we must think again about God's triune nature. The Son suffers dying, and the Father suffers the death of his Son: the fatherlessness of the Son is matched by the sonlessness of the Father. We can almost say that, at the cross, there is in the death of his Son the death of the Father's own fatherhood.

Of course, we must recognise that the Father and the Son's suffering are functionally different – and only Christ's sufferings atone for sin. But this does not mean that we should ignore the Father's infinite grief.

Abraham

It is not really possible to read Romans 8:32 without thinking of Abraham in Genesis 22. The grief of Abraham in preparing to sacrifice Isaac is surely a prophetic glimpse into the grief of 'Abba' as he prepares to abandon his only Son to death.

Genesis 22 ☐

At Calvary, however, there is no-one to intervene and stop the sacrifice, and the Father must proceed and deliver his Son to death as the representative of sinful humanity. Can anyone remotely imagine the Father's pain at hearing his Son's cry in Mark 15:34?

Mark 15:34 ☐

THE PRODIGAL SON

Luke 15:11–32 □

It has often been noted that the parable recorded in Luke 15:11–32 is more about the father than the son – for it is he who is centre stage.

It is clear that the son's repentance is not a condition of the father's love, it is merely the means which enables him to receive his father's love. The father was looking and waiting long before the son's return; and, as soon as he sees the son, without any questions about his motives, he welcomes him with passionate joy.

The main point of the parable is its declaration of the Father's unconditional grace to sinners – and it was part of Jesus' reply to the religious leaders who were criticising him for the same kind of attitude to the same kind of people.

Some people wonder how this parable relates to the cross, because they always think about the cross in terms of the Son's suffering and the cost of grace.

But this is a parable which is spoken by the Son on the way to the cross, and it points us to the centrality of the Father and to the total and lavish freeness of his grace.

In the story, the son returned home with very low expectations. He wondered how his father would react to him. He was not sure whether his father would even speak to him. He assumed that he might have to grovel and beg a great deal, and the best that he hoped was to make some sort of arrangement.

He did not imagine that he might be allowed into the family home, or that he might be allowed to bear the family name, or to have any privileges of sonship. He merely hoped that his father might, in his grace and mercy, accept him as a paid servant.

Through the parable, Jesus declares that the Father is not like this!

Overflowing grace

Many believers have heard much about the cost of redemption and little about the free-and-overflowing grace of the Father who, in his passionate desire for the homecoming of sinners, gave up his only Son.

We do not need to understand redemption to receive forgiveness. We are not required to appreciate the cost of forgiveness before we can benefit from it – we can learn this later.

In fact, the only condition of forgiveness is that we respond to the grace and freedom of the Father with humble, outstretched arms and a thankful, joyful heart. We simply come to the Father, like the son in the story, and take God at his word.

We should remember that if the gospel we preach doesn't seem too good to be true, it probably isn't the gospel!

If we do not look to the Father, if he is not the focus of our faith, if we overlook his part in redemption, there is a possibility of presenting a gospel which suggests that the best people can hope is that the Father can be persuaded into some sort of uncomfortable tolerance of sinners by Jesus.

We may think that returning sons and daughters still need to keep their distance from the Father, and that all our gratitude should be showered upon Jesus for somehow twisting the Father's arm to allow us into a back-room of the family home as the lowest form of servant.

This sort of thinking about the Father leads to passivity, fear, self-condemnation, low expectations, a lack of boldness and legalism.

It might have been how the prodigal son felt while he was trudging home, but it does not represent the father in the parable – or the 'Abba' Father who sent his Son into the far country to make a way home, and who is now waiting with longing to usher us into his presence as sons and daughters with unconditional grace and uninhibited celebration.

To be a believer is to know that the Father has defined our identity through the cross and that he now calls us his sons and daughters. He beckons us to come forward and receive our inheritance – the robe of sonship, the ring of authority, the sandals of freedom.

It is this free grace of the Father which initiates the sending of the Son and sets up redemption – so that, when the price is paid, the Father may open his arms and welcome the multitudes of children who are brought to glory by the Son through the Spirit.

PART SEVEN

the will of the father

We have noted that 'Abba' is a Gethsemane word which is spoken by the Son who trusts his Father so fully that he obeys him completely. For the Son, accepting obedience is the essence of sonship – as we have seen in Matthew 11:25–30; Luke 10:21–22; John 5:19, 30; 6:38; 7:28–29; 8:26, 28–29; 10:18 & 12:49–50.

When we look to Jesus to learn about living as a son or daughter of the Father, we see that it is characterised by total trust and radical obedience. We can say that the sonship of the divine Son clearly consists of obedience – and can therefore expect that the sonship of human children will also consist of obedience.

In *Living Faith*, we note that 'faith', or 'believing', is an almost identical scriptural concept to 'obedience'. To believe in God is to obey him; to obey God is to believe him; and the New Testament uses the words 'faith' and 'obedience' almost interchangeably.

We consider obedient faith throughout *Living Faith*, and all that we learn about obedience in this chapter needs to be understand within the concept of God-given, God-sourced 'living faith'.

Matthew
  11:25–30 ☐

Luke 10:21–22 ☐

John 5:19, 30 ☐
  6:38 ☐
  7:28–29 ☐
  8:26 ☐
  8:28–29 ☐
  10:18 ☐
  12:49–50 ☐

GOSPEL OBEDIENCE

For all sorts of historical, religious and philological reasons, any contemporary stress on obedience sounds hard and foreboding. But the 'gospel obedience', or 'living faith', that we see in Jesus is the exact opposite of 'legalistic obedience'.

The enemy delights to cause us to misunderstand important biblical words, and the common Christian understanding of obedience as 'legalistic' is one of his greatest successes. We need to appreciate that 'gospel obedience' is different, and that it has three main distinguishing elements.

1.   It is a response to God's grace

Gospel obedience is always a response to God's grace and never a condition for grace. (If it were a condition, it could not be grace.) Legalism states that the Father will accept us as children only *if we obey*; whereas the gospel proclaims that the Father welcomes us as returning children exactly as we are, in all our unworthiness, and that our response to the Father's grace is eager obedience.

In Part Six, we saw that returning children are received by the Father without any conditions; but that they return to the Father's home and family where the Father is lord and should be obeyed.

Living in the Father's grace means living in his will; and it is our gospel obedience which keeps us close to him – and to his power, his protection, his provision, his perfection, and so on.

This means that gospel obedience is liberating rather than constricting – because it keeps us in line with the Father's will, which is always a will for our freedom, wholeness and blessing.

John 4:32–34 shows that the Son's obedience was literally the source of his spiritual sustenance, and Jesus' words in John 15:10 follow naturally on from this truth.

Obedience is not a pre-condition of being loved by God. Instead, the Son and the Spirit's perfect love has no better gift for us than to place us in an obedient relationship with the Father who loves us infinitely – so that his love can make us whole and complete.

John 4:32–34 ☐
15:10 ☐

We have noted that the Son lived, died and rose in accepting obedience to the Father's love, and it is when we live with similar acceptance and obedience that we discover a similar joy.

The only true motive behind gospel obedience should be a response of gratitude to the Father's grace – not a fear of punishment. And the only true purpose of gospel obedience should be to maintain us in a position of free and lavish grace – and to draw others to that grace.

As we see in *The Rule of God*, this is why Jesus' words in Matthew 11:25–30 make so much sense – his yoke really is easy and his burden genuinely is light.

Matthew 11:25–30 ☐

2.　It is enabled by God

We can say that gospel obedience is more an enabled obedience than a required obedience. The Father does not make impossible demands and then stand back to watch us fail; instead, he has given us the Son and the Spirit by whom we are enabled to obey him.

We note in *The Rule of God* that the Mosaic Law imposed impossible requirements on Israel which led to failure and condemnation, and that Jesus came to release us from the Law and to replace it with the personal rule of God. We see this throughout Matthew 6–8, and in Romans 8:2.

Romans 8:2 ☐

As believers, we have not been released from all obedience, we have been moved from legal obedience to living faith, to gospel obedience; we have been transferred from the realm of rules and regulations to the personal rule of God. Philippians 2:13 shows how God himself now works in us and with us, by the Spirit, to enable us to act according to his will and purpose.

Philippians 2:13 ☐

3.　It is a personal relationship with God

Gospel obedience is personal living obedience to 'Abba', and not obedience to a code of general principles and detailed regulations. We consider this in detail throughout *The Rule of God*.

Romans 12:1–2 reveals both that self-giving obedience should be our response to God's self-giving, and that – more importantly – it is the means by which we discern, embrace and fulfil the Father's will.

Romans 12:1–2 ☐

It should be plain from Romans 12:1–2 that the whole process of gospel obedience is entirely different from a human attempt to live by Christian principles or to abide by the Ten Commandments – or even to implement the Sermon on the Mount. Whatever we call it – gospel obedience, living faith, or the rule of God – it is undoubtedly *a personal relationship with 'Abba, Father'*.

GOD'S PARTICULAR WILL

As we see in *Knowing the Son*, Jesus continually sought to discern what his Father was doing, and to do that with him. His ministry did not depend on his awareness of godly principles and his ability to apply them; it depended on his sensitivity to the Father's particular will – and this sensitivity was rooted in his intimate relationship with the Father.

Luke 4:18–19 ☐

Of course, there was a general will and purpose for Jesus' life and ministry – it is set out in Luke 4:18–19. But Jesus did not live by a programme or principles; he lived from minute-to-minute by discerning what particular form the consistent will of God was taking in each and every situation. We consider this process of particular will and discernment throughout *Living Faith* and *Listening to God*.

As believers, we do not need divine guidance because we are ignorant of the Father's general will and purpose; we need guidance because we need insight into his particular will in different sets of circumstances.

For example, we know that healing and wholeness are the Father's general-and-ultimate will for all people everywhere, but we need his particular will to know what to say and do when we are confronted by a sick person. If we try to live by general principles without particular insights it is likely that we will live in confusion and disappointment.

We know that it is the Spirit's work to reveal the Father's particular will to us, and that he uses a great variety of means and gifts to do this. We consider the gifts, attributes and guidance of the Holy Spirit in *Knowing the Spirit, Ministry in the Spirit* and *Listening to God*.

Acts 16:6–10 ☐

In Acts 16:6–10, we read how Paul was restrained by the Spirit – first from going one way to preach, and then from going another way

– and how he was finally directed God's particular way. Paul knew that it was the Father's general will for him to preach the gospel to the Gentiles, but he needed the Spirit's help to discern the Father's particular will for his ministry at that time.

It is exactly this sort of 'personally guided, particular obedience' which we need to follow in our lives. We need to listen carefully to the Spirit to discern the Father's particular will in each and every situation – and then we need to obey the Father's will.

'ABBA' OBEDIENCE

Whenever we obey the Father's particular will, we join with Jesus in saying 'Abba' in Gethsemane. The Son's words in Mark 14:36 are the archetype of all particular gospel obedience.

Mark 14:36 ☐

We have seen that Jesus' sonship is not conditional on his obedience; in fact, it is because he knows the Father loves him that he has the confidence – the living faith – to obey. It is this living relationship with the Father which provides Jesus with the strength and freedom to obey.

In Gethsemane, Jesus goes to the Father to test his understanding of God's particular will that he must endure the cross on the morrow. Mark 8:31; 9:31 & 10:33–34 reveal that Jesus already knows God's general will, but he needs the Father's personal reassurance as to his particular will for that night and the following few days.

Mark 8:31 ☐
9:31 ☐
10:33–34 ☐

Father-facing obedience

Jesus' 'Abba' obedience is a God-ward, Father-facing obedience. It is concerned with obeying the Father's will, and not with satisfying his own personal needs and desires.

We live in an age when people constantly seek after instant satisfaction and self-fulfilment, and we need to recognise that these are the antithesis of the 'Abba' prayer in Gethsemane. Of course, we should recognise that our needs often cause us to run to God, and that his grace means he is ready to receive us on the basis of our needs and to meet them.

Jesus' purpose, however, is not just to meet our needs. When we do come to him with our needs, he always seeks to turn us into his disciples – into companions who want to follow him for his sake more than we want to use him to get things for our sake.

We must never forget that Jesus says, 'Come to me and I will send you wherever I choose', and not, 'Come to me and I will give you whatever you want'.

Luke 5:1–11 ☐

We see this process in Luke 5:1–11:

1. *Jesus satisfies the needs of frustrated fishermen.*

2. *Peter moves from a sense of satisfaction at the catch to a sense of sin and unworthiness before Jesus' power.*

3. *Jesus calls Peter to discipleship.*

4. *Jesus sends Peter out to catch people.*

We can say that Peter was converted from a need-based, self-facing relationship to an obedience-based, Father-facing relationship – and that his sense of personal sinfulness was a vital part of the process.

When our faith focuses on our needs, we are doomed to discontentment and disappointment; but when our faith focuses on the Father, we are guaranteed wholeness and completeness.

Of course, we know that Jesus tells those who abide in him and follow him that they will have their needs met. But this is for those who are seeking God's kingdom and righteousness, not for those who are obsessed with their own needs.

True disciples can be trusted with whatever they ask, because what they ask will come out of their relationship with the Father and their alignment with his will. Like Jesus in Gethsemane, they will be asking for the Father's will, and not for their own wants and needs.

Too many believers give in to Jesus' Luke 4:2–3 temptation, and seek for power to satisfy their personal needs. Instead, we need to follow Jesus' Luke 4:4 reply, and live by obeying the word of God.

When we do obey the Father's will with gospel obedience, we will find that our needs are satisfied too.

Spirit-empowered obedience

We have seen that it is the work of the Spirit to sanctify us, to bring us into the likeness of Christ, to enable us to reveal the family 'Name'. And our obedience to the Father's will is crucial if the Spirit is to develop the Father's nature within us.

Spiritual experiences and spiritual gifts are only significant if they express our Gethsemane obedience to the 'Abba' Father – for true gospel obedience is the willingness to follow Jesus from the garden to the cross.

In practice this means being ready, like Jesus in the garden, to:

- *follow in the absence of signs and answers*

- *persevere in dull and difficult circumstances*

- *give way to God's will so that much fruit can grow*

- *defy our fears and witness for Christ – by our words, our lifestyle, and our prophetic response to injustice*

- *be released from the shackles of our needs into the service of others*

- *be humble in the face of the legitimate authority of others*

All this suggests that we will be mighty in the Spirit only when we have been with Jesus in the garden, and have said with him – with deep sincerity – 'Abba Father, not what I will, but what you will'.

THE PRIORITY OF THE FATHER'S WILL

We have seen that the Father's will has priority over our will in his call to obedience. And we know that grace is the Father's initiative, and that gospel obedience is our response to his grace.

The order is clear: the Father initiates, we respond. Before we move one pace towards God, even while we are saying 'No' to him, the Father comes to us in his Son in free-and-lavish grace. Few church leaders would disagree with this order of priority.

When, however, we consider the work of the Spirit, many church leaders strongly disagree with each other about the order of the priority of wills between the Father and his children. For example, many pastors would give quite different answers to these questions.

- *Is the Spirit's action in conversion and anointing free and unconditional, or does he act in us only when we turn to him and ask him and allow him to work?*

- *Do we have faith because the Spirit has come and created that faith, or does he come only when he finds faith already within us?*

- *Does the Spirit actively initiate faith in us, or does he invite us and passively wait for us in our uninfluenced freedom to turn to him?*

These are not hair-splitting academic questions which interest only armchair Christians; they are practical issues which deeply affect the way that every believer relates to the Father and lives the Christian life.

Can the human will have priority over the Father's will?

Since the time of John Wesley, it has been popular in many Protestant churches to claim that all God's actions in us are conditioned by our willingness and faith. Many leaders teach that the Father cannot bring the blessing of the Son and the Spirit until we have, by our own free will, opened the way for him to do so.

As a result of this idea, many evangelistic sermons appeal to human free will as the decisive factor in whether or not people are saved. When this is pushed too far, it can seem as though, at the pivotal moment, God suddenly becomes inactive and unable to help – he has to stand passively aside while we decide whether or not we will get saved.

People apply the same idea to receiving the Spirit and his gifts. They suggest that Jesus cannot anoint us with the Spirit until we have fulfilled the conditions which God has laid down.

If we know enough, believe enough, repent enough, pray enough, seek enough, attend the course and buy the video, then, in the end, we will be anointed. If we fulfil the conditions, God will pour out his blessing. But if we don't, he won't. In this way of thinking, the human will has priority, not the Father's will.

Quite simply, every believer must decide whether they believe that the divine order is; 'grace-then-obedience', or 'obedience-then-grace'. Whichever approach we choose, we then rigorously apply our choice to every aspect of the faith.

It should be obvious that, throughout this *Sword of the Spirit* series, we have sought to show that the Father's will always has priority; that grace is either always first-and-foremost or it ceases to be grace; that God's faith, the Spirit's anointing, the gifts and ministries of the Spirit, are all given essentially in the context of the Father's free-and-lavish grace. Any divine conditions – like, for example, gospel obedience – are our grateful response to grace, not requirements for grace.

Infinite grace

The difficulty we face today is that, in large parts of pentecostalism and charismatic evangelicalism, grace appears to play a part only in conversion, and rarely features in other aspects of the Christian life.

'Obedience-then-grace' is at the heart of much contemporary teaching. This means that those who are hungry for renewal and revival turn to techniques, systems and methods instead of to God's free promise and grace.

If we believe that the Father's will has priority in all things, that his grace is infinite-and-absolute, we will turn to him when we are spiritually hungry. But if we believe that our will has priority, that it is 'obedience-then-grace', we will turn to the latest methods which are guaranteed to bring us into blessing if we follow them carefully.

We should ask ourselves what sort of Father we have.

- Is he the *Yahweh Elohim* whom we have considered, who is all-powerful, all-protecting, all-perfect and all-providing; whose great passion is our redemption; who has suffered the infinite grief of love; who has revealed his eternal love by giving his only Son for us; who keeps on coming to us in the Son and the Spirit; who delights to give us good things?

- Or is he one who has tossed his blessings onto a table and told us to come and get them – if we can – and then left us to work our own way through an almost impossible maze of right and wrong approaches?

How are God's promises fulfilled?

One of the most burning questions for every believer to answer is how God's promises are fulfilled. We need to decide whether it is:

1. *by our working through a list of conditions, and then performing a series of actions which match them*

2. *by the Father in his grace leading us step-by-step towards the receiving of them – in his way and at his time*

If we are convinced that it is the second, we will never follow a method or formula. Instead, we will always look only to the Father, and watch what he is doing, and follow him in the way he is taking.

Luke 11:13 □

Jesus' promise in Luke 11:13 is very important in this context. He promises that, 'Your heavenly Father is willing to give the Holy Spirit to those who ask him.'

There are two main elements in the verse:

*   *the Father's willingness*

*   *our asking*

We can relate these two elements to each other in contrasting ways.

1. The Father's willingness is conditioned by our asking. He is willing to give, when and as much as we ask. If we do not ask, he will not give.

2. Our asking is conditioned by the Father's willingness. It is only because he is willing that we dare to ask. It is the power of his Word at work in us which gives us the power to ask. (We consider this in Part Four of *Living Faith*.)

    This means that the Spirit is not merely the gift who comes at the end of our asking, he is also there at the beginning – the creator of our desire, the strength of our seeking, the boldness of our approaching, and so on, ad infinitum.

There is real human asking in both these approaches. In the first, it is before God's will, and is a condition of his willingness to give. In the second, it is the result and outworking of God's will to give.

Believers who apply the first approach to the promise of salvation think that repentance is the condition of grace, and that they turn to God to receive his forgiveness. Whereas those who apply the second

THE WILL OF THE FATHER

approach believe that repentance is the result of grace, and that they turn to him because he has already forgiven them in grace and mercy.

Those who favour the first approach, and want to experience spiritual renewal, will feel that *they* must work hard at their prayer-lives, their believing, their purity, and so on: they will generally be characterised by considerable self-effort.

Those, however, who prefer the second approach, will believe that the Father, in his grace, begins by his Spirit to renew them – step-by-step – into the faith, purity and praying which are his will for them and the signs of his grace within them. It is not that he forces these things upon us – as some caricature this approach – rather, it is that he gives a new freedom and will so that we are ready and able to receive them.

THE FATHER'S WILL

We have seen that there are leaders who insist that there must be a human initiative in the realisation or appropriation of redemption. But we should recognise just how strongly Ephesians 1:4–6 asserts that the initiative is entirely with the Father.

Ephesians 1:4–6 ☐

Many preachers are concerned to 'challenge' people to respond to the gospel – and the assumption behind their challenge is the idea that fallen people are capable of making a positive response. But we should grasp just how forcibly Ephesians 2:1–5 denies that fallen people have any such capability – unless God restores it to them in Christ and creates it in them by the Spirit.

Ephesians 2:1–5 ☐

Those who affirm the order 'obedience-then-grace' consider that believers make a significant contribution to their salvation and blessing by fulfilling the conditions and deciding to believe the promise. But we should appreciate the unequivocal nature of Ephesians 2:8–9.

Ephesians 2:8–9 ☐

We see in *Living Faith* that the saving faith through which God blesses us is itself his gracious gift to us – and not our work that we bring to him as our contribution to the redemptive process.

There is simply no room for any smugness or boasting when we finally appreciate the absolute priority of the Father's will and the

Ephesians 2:10 □

eternal-and-infinite extent of his grace. The most that we can do is to recite Ephesians 2:10. Of course, we need to work out our salvation and live in partnership with the Spirit (as we make clear *in The Rule of God*, *Living Faith* and *Knowing the Spirit*); but we are only able to do this as God works in us.

Many churches long for renewal and revival, but these come when we despair of our competence to fulfil anything, when we turn to the Father to see what he wills to do by his grace, and when we wait obediently for him to lead us into his promises.

The gracious will of the Father is the only originating source of all blessings, and everything in our faith stems from his grace. But we should not forget that his free and infinite grace calls us to respond to the Father with grateful and unconditional Gethsemane obedience. Grace-then-obedience is surely the only route into the glorious freedom of the sons and daughters of the Father.

PART EIGHT

the father and prayer

Throughout this book, we have learnt much about the glorious name and nature of our triune God, and we have learnt even more about the first person of God, about the Father.

We have stressed repeatedly that we are called to know the Father personally, and not just to know facts about him. And now we should begin to appreciate that we develop our personal 'knowing-and-known' relationship with the Father as we draw near to him in prayer.

When God is called Father in the New Testament, it is usually within a context of prayer, worship or glorification. We see this, for example, in Matthew 5:16; 6:6; 11:25; 26:39, 53; Luke 10:21; 11:2; 23:34; John 11:41; 12:28; 14:16; 17:1, 5, 11, 26; Romans 8:15; 2 Corinthians 1:3; Ephesians 1:3; 2:18; 3:14; 5:20; Philippians 4:20; Colossians 1:3, 12; 3:17; James 3:9; 1 Peter 1:3, 17 and Revelation 1:6.

This will not surprise us when we realise both that the word 'Abba' goes back to the climax of Jesus' prayer life in Mark 14:3, and that approaching God as Father is central to Jesus' prayer teaching in Luke 11:1–13.

Matthew 5:16 ☐
6:6 ☐
11:25 ☐
26:39, 53 ☐

Luke 10:21 ☐
11:2 ☐
23:34 ☐

John 11:41 ☐
12:28 ☐
14:16 ☐
17:1–26 ☐

Romans 8:15 ☐

2 Corinthians 1:3 ☐

Ephesians 1:3 ☐
2:18 ☐
3:14 ☐
5:20 ☐

Philippians 4:20 ☐

Colossians 1:3 ☐
1:12 ☐
3:17 ☐

James 3:9 ☐

1 Peter 1:3, 17 ☐

Revelation 1:6 ☐

Mark 14:36 ☐

Luke 11:1–13 ☐

TRINITARIAN PRAYER

The Son's teaching about prayer in Luke 11 begins with a prayer which is addressed to the Father and concludes with an invitation to pray for the Holy Spirit – whom the Father is willing to give to those who ask.

We need the Spirit

The context of Luke 11:1–12 suggests that the Luke 11:13 asking for the Spirit is actually a prayer for the empowering of prayer, as it is only in the Spirit that we can pray with reality.

The New Testament teaches two important truths which have enormous implications for prayer and worship:

Galatians 4:6 □

- *we can call God 'Father' only when we are in the Spirit* – Galatians 4:6

Ephesians
5:18–19 □

- *we can praise the Father's name only when we are filled with the Spirit* – Ephesians 5:18–19

We should not think that the Luke 11:13 prayer to the Father implies that the Spirit has previously been absent. It simply means that the Spirit who comes is not 'our' possession, that he is not at 'our' beck-and-call: we consider the Spirit's 'untameable' nature as 'the wind of God' in *Effective Prayer* and *Knowing the Spirit*.

The main thrust of Luke 11:1–13 is that we need to keep on praying, to keep on asking, to depend each day on God's provision for that day. It is 'particular prayer' and 'particular provision' – rather like the 'particular will' and 'particular guidance' we considered in Part Seven.

Like most of Luke 11, verse 13 uses a special Greek tense, and it can be translated something like this, 'Your heavenly Father goes on being willing to keep on giving the Holy Spirit to those who go on asking him'.

The Father is willing to keep on pouring the Spirit onto-and-into us, to keep on empowering-and-enabling us for prayer. And our grateful daily response to his gracious daily willingness-and-initiative should be to keep on asking him for the Spirit – so that we keep on being enabled to keep on approaching the Father in prayer.

Luke 11:1–13 demonstrates that Christian prayer is thoroughly trinitarian. It is addressed:

- *to the Father*

- *through the Son*

- *in the Spirit*

In prayer, we face the Father and relate to him. But our only way to him is through Jesus who teaches us to pray. And our ability to pray is itself a gift in-and-of the Holy Spirit. This is set out clearly in Ephesians 2:18.

Ephesians 2:18 ☐

1.   To the Father

As we read the New Testament, it is plain that God the Father should be the primary focus of prayer.

Our prayer, our praise, our worship, our thanks, our glorification, and so on, may sometimes be directed to Jesus and to the Spirit – because they also are God; they share his being and nature, and deserve to be equally praised and adored.

But the whole movement of the life of God – both as Creator and Redeemer – has its source and its goal in the Father. The Son and the Spirit are themselves from the Father and for the Father, so that their chief aim in prayer is to introduce us to the Father and to establish us in fellowship with him.

It follows naturally from this, and from the main purpose of the gospel, that most of our prayers should properly be addressed to the Father. We cannot pray apart from the Son and the Spirit, and they both teach us to pray, 'Abba Father'.

Despite this, many believers address most of their prayers to Jesus. This suggests an incomplete understanding both of the gospel and of the Father.

If we pray habitually to Jesus we are overlooking the truth that Jesus came as the way to the Father. We need to ask ourselves whether we are concentrating on the incarnate Son because we think that the Father is essentially transcendent, unapproachable and unknowable. And whether we are clinging to a kind and loving Jesus because we think that we need him to placate a remote and still angry Father.

Whether they realise it or not, when believers pray mainly *to* Jesus rather than *through* him, or mainly *to* the Spirit rather than *in* him, they are casting doubts on their relationship with the Father. This is not just a matter of semantics, for it cuts to the heart of the gospel.

As we have seen, the gospel is the gospel of the Father: through Christ, we are reconciled with the infinite-and-eternal love which is the Father. If we forget this, we will always be affected in some way by fear. But if we grasp the ultimate purpose of the gospel, we will realise that we have been reconciled with the Father – so that we can know him, and the assurance and wholeness which comes from living in his good-and-perfect will.

John 16:26–28 ☐

When we appreciate this, we will confidently approach *the Father* in prayer. John 16:26–28 contains the central message of the gospel – that the Father loves us. This is the main thrust of all Jesus' teaching; it is the principle revelation of the Spirit; and we are not living in it until we are boldly approaching the centre of all things knowing that we are welcome and are *enabled* to say, 'Abba Father'.

2.   Through the Son

John 16:26–28 reveals that, in prayer, Jesus *mediates* with the Father on our behalf. There are two different types of mediation and we need to be clear which of these Jesus practices.

- *exclusive mediation* – a mediator goes for us where we cannot go, and does for us what we cannot do

- *inclusive mediation* – a mediator goes for us so that we can follow after, and do what we could not do before

Jesus' ministry in prayer does not mean that he goes to the Father for us because we cannot approach the Father for ourselves. Instead, Jesus has pioneered the way to the Father for us so that we can go to the Father *with him*.

Hebrews 4:16 ☐

We do not come to the Father *by ourselves*, but we do come to the Father ourselves *with-and-through the Son*. We see this idea of mediation in Hebrews 4:16.

This means that prayer is not something we do out of ourselves. It is something we do because of Jesus – through him, and in him, and with him – and so that, in the Spirit, direct face-to-face fellowship is established with the Father and we can personally offer him our thanks, our praise, our intercessions, and all the other forms of prayer we consider in *Effective Prayer*.

This type of mediation has obvious pastoral implications for all church leaders and ministers. If the Son mediates with the Father to include us rather than to exclude us, to share access rather than to deny it, we need to ensure that all Christ's ministries and ministers follow the same principle.

We know that Christ has appointed different ministries and ministers within his church. These are not meant to stand between people and God, they are meant to help people to come to the Father for themselves. For example, when a needy person asks us to pray for them, we should ensure that we follow Christ in praying *with them* rather than *instead of them*.

And when we minister something like healing, we should not try to deal with God on a person's behalf; instead, we should stir up their faith so that they can receive their healing as a personal gift from the Father, rather than as an indirect gift which has come via ourselves. Most of the misplaced adulation of ministers is based in a misunderstanding of Christ's ministry of mediation.

We need to ensure that expressions like 'let me pray for you' do not mean 'let me pray instead of you'. We must not give the impression that we are thinking, 'Let me go where you cannot go, where I will be heard and you will not'. This sort of thinking undermines people's confidence in the Father and communicates a false impression of him and his gospel. This is not how Jesus speaks in John 16:26.

John 16:26 ☐

Instead, we should use words like, 'let me pray with you' and clearly offer to support people as we go together through Christ to the Father. This is the biblical *inclusive* view of ministry – and it helps us to appreciate the relevance and potency of verses like Matthew 18:20.

Matthew 18:20 ☐

3.   In the Spirit

We see in *Effective Prayer* that the 'praying in the Spirit' described in Ephesians 2:18 and 6:18 is not some special form of prayer – like tongues – or some especially intense times of prayer (though it does include these).

Ephesians 2:18 ☐
6:18 ☐

Instead, the term, 'prayer in the Spirit' refers to all true prayer – through the Son, to the Father – which depends on the Spirit for power, enabling and direction.

Prayer in the Spirit is not something we can do on our own, in our own strength, experience and ability. Rather, it is a human activity which is enabled, empowered and directed by being caught up into the eternal relationship between the three uni-persons of God.

In the Spirit, we are still fully ourselves. We pray to the Father using our humans thoughts and words – knowing that he affirms and accepts us. But, as we pray, we share in the relationship of the Father, the Spirit and the Son so that we are not left alone to struggle to gain God's attention by own human efforts. Romans 8:26–27 describes how the Spirit helps us, and we consider this fully in *Knowing the Spirit* and *Effective Prayer*.

Romans 8:26–27 ☐

THE LORD'S PRAYER

Luke 11:2–4 ☐

We have already noted the radical way that the Lord's prayer approaches God as Father, but here we need to consider Jesus' prayer in Luke 11:2–4 a little more deeply.

Jewish liturgy

In many ways, Jesus' prayer is closely related to Jewish prayers of his day. The first two clauses are very similar to a common prayer which was used at the end of most synagogue sermons to ask for the hallowing of God's name and the coming of God's kingdom.

By building on this widely-accepted liturgical root, Jesus shows that he does not reject the worship of the people around him; instead, he accepts it, embraces it, uses it and renews it.

While it is true that Jesus' identification of God as 'Our Father' transforms the way that his disciples approach God, his use of traditional Jewish liturgy both underlines his inclusiveness and shows that the Father can be approached liturgically as well as spontaneously.

Contemporary language

In Jesus' day, most Jewish prayers were spoken in Hebrew, the special holy language of formal worship; but Jesus' prayers used Aramaic – the ordinary language of the common people.

At that time, people believed that God was too special to be addressed in 'the common tongue'. But Jesus' prayers demonstrate that the Father is too close to be addressed in archaic language. He is the living God of today, and needs to be addressed in the language of today – even if a liturgical framework is used.

By using Aramaic, Jesus removed prayer from the world of sacred language and placed it in the middle of everyday life. This has obvious implications for those believers who think that 'reverence' means we should use seventeenth century English and archaic expressions whenever we approach the Father in prayer.

The disciples' prayer

The Lord's prayer is a particular prayer for the followers of Jesus. At that time, different religious groups were identified by distinctive forms of prayer. And the disciples wanted Jesus to follow John the Baptist's example and give them a particular prayer which would express the essence of their life together. We see this in Luke 11:1.

We already know that the distinctive thing which Jesus' disciples had to learn was that they were to call God 'Our Father' whenever they approached him in prayer.

Today, many people think of the Lord's prayer as a general, 'neutral' prayer which is suitable for anyone to pray. It was very different in the early church, for the Lord's prayer and the Lord's supper were the two central elements of early Christian worship. They were reserved for those who were fully committed to Christ and were not disclosed to those who were outside the church.

The right to pray the Lord's prayer was reserved for those who were in Christ – because the early church understand it to be a prayer which only redeemed disciples could pray, for only they knew God as 'Father'.

Each petition in Jesus' Luke 11 teaches us something important about approaching the Father in prayer.

Hallowed be your name

We should now be able to appreciate the depth of meaning in this simple petition. The magnificent breadth of meaning in the Old Testament teaching about God's name is summarised in the one word 'Father', and we must hallow every aspect of God's name and nature, and glorify his essential fatherhood.

The Greek word *hagiazo* is translated as 'hallow', but it comes from *hagios* – holy – and literally means 'sanctify' or 'set apart'. This petition merely restates what we already know from the Old Testament, that God's name is holy – and should be treated as such.

This 'hallowing' involves *guarding God's name* from misuse and false-impression. At times, this means dealing with blasphemy and bad language; more commonly, it means not using his name to make false claims.

Every time someone says 'God told me', when they are merely offering their human opinion or making a banal observation, God's name is misused because his omniscient nature is implicitly slandered.

More positively, 'hallowing' involves *rejoicing in God's name*. This means shifting our emphasis in prayer towards praise and thanksgiving. We see this in the openings and endings of Paul's letters, and we develop this in *Worship in Spirit and Truth*.

Human-centred prayer and worship is inevitably dominated by confession, petition and intercession – it revolves around our sins and needs. But 'Father-hallowing' worship is characterised by praise, worship and thanksgiving. We hallow God's name when we move from 'Bless me' to 'Bless the Father' – because we make him central.

Your kingdom come, your will be done

Praise prepares us for the next phrase, which urges us to seek the Father's kingdom rule. This underlines that the spiritual process really is 'grace-then-obedience'. God's kingdom comes, and we then respond to his personal will with grateful obedience.

We consider God's kingdom throughout *The Rule of God*, and note that the kingdom is both 'now and not yet'. It has come in Christ; it keeps on coming in signs and wonders as a manifestation of the king, but it still has to come in all fullness.

We have noted that this phrase seems to be based in a common synagogue prayer; but Jesus' declaration that the kingdom has come would have enabled his disciples to pray this with far more confidence than their Jewish contemporaries.

Our experience that the kingdom – God's personal rule – keeps on coming means that we can pray it with equal confidence. And our awareness that the kingdom will come in its fullness (when and how God wills) ensures that we can pray it with absolute hope.

Give us day by day our daily bread

We can say that Jesus' prayer begins by focusing on God's 'perfection'; that it then concentrates on his 'power'; then on his 'provision', and finally on his 'protection'.

This illustrates how Jesus' prayer relates to the Old Testament understanding of God's name. Truly 'Our Father' is himself 'the Name' – he is *El Qodesh*, *Yahweh Sabaoth*, *El Shaddai*, *El Elyon*, and all the other divine names that we have considered.

This phrase addresses God's provision; but we should note the progression – it is not the first request. When we are hungry for God's holiness, righteousness and kingdom *first*, we find that he adds our needs to these things. This is why praise and thanksgiving which glorify and honour God's divine name should precede petition and intercession which deal with our human needs.

It is not fully clear what 'daily bread' means. It could mean:

- *the physical food which is absolutely necessary for that day*

- *the spiritual food which is absolutely necessary for that day*

- *physical food for tomorrow*

- *spiritual food for tomorrow*

- *the spiritual food which we need for the Great Tomorrow*

- *all of the above*

The truth is that the Father provides what his children need for their bodies *and* their spirits; and his present provision is always a 'first instalment', a 'foreshadowing', of what he will provide at the last day.

John 6:10–14 ☐
6:27–40 ☐

We see this in John 6, where Jesus feeds the immediate physical hunger of the crowds, *and* provides twelve baskets of food for the morrow, *and* offers himself as the bread of life which the Father gives to meet our ultimate hunger.

Forgive us our sins, for we forgive everyone who is indebted to us

This is another important phrase which demonstrates the truth of the 'grace-then-obedience' order. We should forgive others as a grateful response to God's gracious forgiveness, not as a pre-condition for receiving his forgiveness!

Luke 5:8 ☐

Once again, we need to note the order in Jesus' prayer. We do not approach the Father riddled with guilt and begging for forgiveness so that we can put our requests to him. Instead, like Peter in Luke 5:8, we see our need for forgiveness and cleansing *when* we have praised the Father, have sought the grace of his kingdom, and have depended completely on his provision.

By using this order, Jesus teaches his disciples not to be obsessed with their sin and unworthiness; but rather to be aware of them, and to ask the Father to deal with them – knowing that his grace guarantees that he will.

Do not lead us into temptation, but deliver us from the evil one

Jesus' prayer ends with a request for sanctification. This is to be prayed by those who are proceeding along the path to holiness – to the family likeness – but are finding that the way has many traps and distractions.

The Greek word *peirasmos* is better understood as 'testing' rather than 'temptation', and refers to those inward temptations and outward trials which test our faith.

We should also realise that this is a prayer for God's active protection and deliverance. The petition means 'Cause us not to give in to testing' rather than, 'Do not cause us to give in to testing'.

It would be a strange serpent-sending Father who needed to be implored to stop making his children fall into temptation. Instead, *El Elyon* himself is 'our Father, our Redeemer'. He will (and he wills to) deliver us from all the snares of the evil one.

He is the good Father of Luke 11:13, who is willing to give the Holy Spirit – the all-in-all of all the petitions in the prayer, the ultimate good thing, the very being and presence and person of the Father himself – to all those who gratefully ask him in prayer.

Luke 11:13 ☐

PART NINE

our father

In the first three chapters of this book, we tried to develop a panoramic picture of the name, nature and fatherhood of the triune God, and sought to gain an over-all picture of the biblical revelation about God. We learnt about *Yahweh Elohim*, the 'one, but more-than-one' being who is the Creator, Redeemer and Father of all things.

In the following three chapters, we focused on the first person of God, on the Father, and sought to gain an over-all picture of him as the Scriptures reveal him in his eternal relationships with the second and third uni-persons of God. We learnt about *Abba*, the heavenly Father of our Lord Jesus Christ.

Then, in the last two chapters, we concentrated on our personal, intimate relationship with the Father, and sought to establish what this means practically for our everyday lives. We learnt that we are called to respond to the Father's grace with unceasing gospel obedience and Spirit-inspired prayer.

Finally, in this last chapter, we need to appreciate that God is essentially 'Our' Father rather than 'My' Father.

THE FATHER, THE CREATOR

We have already noted in Part Three that the New Testament presents three aspects of God's fatherhood. He is:

- *the redemptive Father of all believers*

- *the unique Father of Jesus*

- *the universal Father of all humanity*

We have considered in some detail the truth that God is the Father of all believers and all disciples, and have seen that this aspect of God's fatherhood is the result of his redemptive activity.

We have also established the truth that Jesus is 'God's only Son'; and have realised that this implicitly points to God's unique fatherhood of his unique Son Jesus.

But, thus far, we have paid little attention to the truth that God is the Father of all people and all nations.

Matthew 5:45 and Luke 6:35 show that God's fatherly attributes are displayed even to 'the unthankful and the evil'; and Jesus presents God as universal Father throughout the Sermon on the Mount; but he also clearly sets God's universal fatherhood in the context of God as Creator. This is particularly plain in Matthew 5:43–48 & 6:25–34.

Matthew 5:45 ☐
Luke 6:35 ☐

Father *and* Creator

We know that the God who is the Father of his children is also the Creator of the whole world, and we can truly appreciate him as 'Our' Father only when we relate his fatherhood to his creatorship.

As redeemed believers, our personal 'known-and-knowing' relationships with the Father – through the Son and in the Spirit – are set within the wider context of God's total purpose for all creation. Unless we have some understanding of this universal setting, we will not fully appreciate *what* and *why* God wills to do in-and-through us.

When we concentrate on God as Creator, we instinctively recognise that he is the origin and source of all things. And when we focus on him as Father, we realise that his universal purpose for all things is to draw everything together into sonship and daughtership.

When we concentrate on God as Creator we look back at the beginning and see what his perfect will has always been for the world. And when we focus on him as Father we look forward to the end and see his ultimate purpose for creation.

If we put this another way, we can say that when we think about God as Creator we dwell on his responsibility for the whole world; and that when we think about him as Father we delight in his redeemed and reconciled relationships with his children. Clearly, we need to hold both ideas together at all times.

When we do keep these insights together, we can see that the Creator exercises his divine responsibility by aiming to draw all people into a family relationship with the Son (through whom his fatherly love is perfectly revealed) and to fill them with the Spirit (in whom we can relate to him as Father and respond to him as children).

In Christ, the Creator has made an open door to God's house for the whole world. But not all men and women have yet entered into the family home to enjoy their rightful relationship with the Father.

All this means that, whenever we use the expression 'Our' Father, we are implicitly acknowledging that it is the Father's will and purpose for *all created men and women* to live in grateful gospel obedience as his redeemed children.

God's 'our' fatherhood is easy to appreciate in the essential corporate nature of the church, which we stress in *Glory in the Church*. Involvement with the world-wide company of redeemed believers helps to move us on from *my* Father towards *our* Father; but we also need to recognise God's fatherly purpose for the whole world.

THE WORLD OF THE FATHER

We have noted that we hold our privileges as children of the Father in trust for the rest of the world. And we have recognised the great hope of the New Testament that, one day, the fullness of both the Gentiles and Israel will be brought into the family of God. We glimpse these in Romans 11:25–27; 1 Corinthians 15:20–28; Revelation 4:11; 5:9–13.

Romans
    11:25–27 ☐

1 Corinthians
    15:20–28 ☐

Revelation 4:11 ☐
    5:9–13 ☐

When we think about the work of the Son and the Spirit, it is easy to focus almost exclusively on matters like conversion, renewal and church life. But we need to appreciate that the Father, the Son and the Spirit are concerned with every aspect of creation, with the whole universe in all its physical and social realities.

John 3:16 declares that God so loved the whole world, the entire *kosmos*, that he gave his Son for it; and this suggests that we may need to think about salvation in bigger ways than we do.

By the time of Christ, the whole world was in the power of the evil one – and this affected every dimension of created life. And John 12:31 shows that Christ's resurrection victory was over everything to do with the world. His judgement was not just over individual sin, it was also over sinful social structures, sinful governments, and the whole sin-spoilt created order.

Jesus did not save the world by destroying it; he re-created it and made it possible for the world to have a right relationship with the Father. Jesus' resurrection body did not abolish the physical realm; it possessed the same physical structure which the Father had originally given, perfectly fulfilled his original purpose for all humanity, and passed into a new quality of life and freedom.

This shows that God's purpose in redemption, through Christ, affirms the world, but it also fundamentally re-aligns it. We see this in Ephesians 1:10.

The first-fruit of the new creation

1 Corinthians 15:45 reveals that the risen Christ, the ultimate human, is the Father-willed destiny of all creation. He has attained the original-and-ultimate purpose of God for which all people were created; and he exists in a perfect relationship with his Father, with his brothers and sisters, and with all the structures and resources of the whole world.

When the life of the risen Christ is reflected, by the Spirit, in the life of his people, the church itself becomes the sign, the 'first-fruits', of the renewed and re-aligned creation. We see this in 2 Corinthians 4:6, and consider it more fully in *Glory in the Church*.

This means that, as the church is renewed by the Spirit into the likeness of Christ, so the life of the church becomes increasingly

John 3:16 ☐
12:31 ☐

Ephesians 1:10 ☐

1 Corinthians
15:45 ☐

2 Corinthians 4:6 ☐

important to the whole world. Romans 8:22–23 makes plain the relevance of a renewed church for the whole creation – for the Father's world is groaning and travailing in frustration until the children of God begin to come into their own.

Romans 8:22–23 ☐

The prophetic revelation of God's wisdom

Ephesians 3:10–11 declares that God's present intention is for the church to make his wisdom known to the 'principalities and powers' – according to his eternal purpose which he accomplished in Christ.

Ephesians
  3:10–11 ☐

The Greek word *exousia* is sometimes translated as 'powers' and at other times as 'authorities'. The Bible teaches that these *exousia*:

- *were created by God* – Colossians 1:16

Colossians 1:16 ☐

- *rule over men and women who are disobedient* – Ephesians 2:2

Ephesians 2:2 ☐

- *hold people in demonic servitude* – Colossians 2:20; Galatians 4:3

Colossians 2:20 ☐

Galatians 4:3 ☐

- *seek to separate us from God's love* – Romans 8:38

Romans 8:38 ☐

- *crucified the Lord of glory* – 1 Corinthians 2:6–8

1 Corinthians
  2:6–8 ☐

- *were triumphed over by the cross* – Colossians 2:15

Colossians 2:15 ☐

These verses suggest that Paul's phrase 'principalities and powers' refers to demonic authorities which influence, dominate and control all the structures of the world. We must note, however, that not every New Testament use of *exousia* refers to demonic authorities; Romans 13:1, for example, clearly points to human authorities rather than to any 'powers' behind them.

Romans 13:1 ☐

Many church leaders believe that there are a variety of religious powers, intellectual powers, moral powers and political powers in the world. The church is not meant to be in bondage to any of these powers/structures/authorities, because Christ has stripped them of their power. Instead, the church is meant to reveal God's wisdom to them, and to show them how they can be renewed and re-aligned by the Spirit into the different structures of the new creation.

This means that the church – the 'Our' Father people – is meant to be a first-fruit, a sample, of the kind of new creation humanity within which, for example, racial, economic, sexual and political differences have been surmounted.

This prophetic role of the church is vital for the whole world. Some believers miss it because they reject the world and allow it to remain captive to the demonic forces of society. Others miss it because they do not grasp the Father's heart and purpose for the whole of creation.

We, however, must be those who affirm the world, who are aware of demonic powers, and who prophetically reveal God's manifold wisdom to *all* creation.

Individual believers and individual churches relate to God as 'Our' Father both by being rooted in their personal relationship with the Father, *and* also by expressing themselves practically in a way which prophetically challenges the oppressive structures of the society within which they live.

When local churches overcome the sociological distinctions between rich and poor, educated and uneducated, old and young, black and white, and so on, they become a relevant sign to the groaning world around them of the Creator's new creation and the Father's family life.

Many pentecostal and charismatic Christians focus on the personal dimension of demonic beings, and concentrate on casting spirits from individual needy people. We should, however, be equally concerned with the sociological dimension of demonic *exousia*, with our hurting world, and should seek God for gracious signs to disarm and overthrow the *exousia* too.

Only a first-fruit

We know that the kingdom is 'now and not yet'. The church has only the first-fruit of the kingdom, just as it has only the first-fruit of the Spirit. But it does have the first-fruit, and we can be a credible sign of the kingdom to the Father's groaning world.

For example, local churches can:

- *break the tyranny of religious rules and traditions, and find those ways of worship which are pleasing to the Spirit and culturally relevant to the world*

- *lead its members into a new dynamic of family life which is more effective and eloquent then negative denunciations of unbiblical ways of living*

- *experiment with forms of community living which meet the needs of single, elderly and needy people*

- *pioneer ways of living which express solidarity with brothers and sisters in poorer nations and in poorer parts of our own nation*

- *practise financial fellowship which prophetically addresses our mammon-dominated society*

- *relate in humility and service to other local churches in a way which magnifies the gospel message of reconciliation and demonstrates the oneness of Christ's body*

Gospel obedience urges us on, but the demonic powers of our cultural background and way-of-life hold us back. Many believers feel a need for personal renewal, but are less sure about the renewal of our Father's world and society.

Many believers take steps forward in obedience to some things, but hesitate when they could become locally and nationally prophetic – as opposed to just being individually prophetic.

Sometimes, even, the evil one directs a church's enthusiasm into the relative safety of personal evangelism because he is terrified of them becoming a truly prophetic community which says and does something which matters to the groaning world around them.

As we approach the end of this book, we must decide whether we will move on from 'My' Father to 'Our' Father; whether we will move on in gospel obedience to the Father who wants to make us a prophetic sign to his hurting world of the renewing, re-aligning power of the Son.

THE FATHER OF THE WORLD

Ephesians 3:14–15 reveals the Father as the Lord of all creation. We are called to bow our knees to the Father from whom the whole family in heaven and earth derives its name.

Ephesians
3:14–15 ☐

The Greek word *patria*, which is translated as family, has a much wider meaning than our modern understanding of the nuclear family. It can mean tribe, family, nation and race; and it refers to the real relationship structures of our created existence in the 'more-than-one' corporate image of God.

This means that every aspect of society has real meaning and significance only in relation to God the Father. Every structure of society – individual, marriage, family, tribe, nation, and so on – has been created by the Father; and what they are all truly meant to be is revealed only when we live in our marriages, homes, schools, factories, churches, clubs, ethnic groups, nations, world, and so on, in trust and gospel obedience to the Father.

It is surely significant that this statement in Ephesians 3:14, about the relationship of society to the Father, is the introduction to a prayer for spiritual renewal and revival.

It is as though Paul is reminding us of the world context of being strengthened with the power of the Spirit – so that we can grasp every dimension of God's love for our whole society.

This means that the Father's will in Christ extends to the renewal and re-alignment of everything that he has made, to the transformation of creation to be the home of transformed humanity, to the rescue of the created structures of life from the demonic powers which control them.

Just as the fall of the first humans meant the bondage and frustration of all creation, so the revelation of the ultimate human means the liberation of all creation – in every form of its life.

Quite simply, it is the Father's good will that local churches, with all their different 'Father-facing' members and structures, and as they reflect the love of the Father in the Spirit, should be the prophetic sign which confronts and challenges their part of the Father's world and draws people to 'Our Father' and into his glorious family.

ACTIVITIES for individuals and small groups

who is god?

Why are contemporary beliefs like 'atheism' and 'humanism' essentially spiritual ideas, and not intellectual constructions?

....

....

....

....

God cannot be proved or disproved by philosophical argument or scientific enquiry: he can be known only through a spiritual revelation which is received by faith. Christian thinkers, however, have proposed four main philosophical arguments for God's existence.

What are these arguments? Briefly explain them, as if to an unbeliever.

1.   ....

....

....

2.   ....

....

....

3.   ....

....

....

4.   ....

....

....

The Bible consistently explains who God is by revealing his nature and character. Instead of defining God, it introduces him: it reveals him personally, not propositionally. Rather than offering abstract facts about God, the Bible presents him in the context of relationships with ordinary people.

How does Psalm 139 reveal God?

....

What does Psalm 139 reveal about God?

....

....

....

....

....

THE BEING AND ATTRIBUTES OF GOD

God's 'eternity' is the most basic biblical idea about God – and a right understanding of God hinges on appreciating the consequences of his eternal nature.

What do these passages teach about the eternal nature of God? Genesis 21:33; Numbers 23:9; Deuteronomy 33:27; 1 Samuel 15:29; Psalm 48:14; 90:1–2; Isaiah 40:28; 57:15; Malachi 3:6; James 1:17.

....

....

....

What does 'the eternity of God' mean for aspects of God's nature like love, power, grace, knowledge and mercy?

....

....

Why is it more accurate to speak about God being 'the source of life' rather than 'alive'?

....

....

What does Isaiah 57:15 teach about God?

....

....

What does John 4:24 teach about God?

....

What, practically, does this mean for you?

....

How do these verses show that God is personal? Genesis 1:27; Numbers 25:3; Psalm 103:13; Isaiah 40:13–14; Hosea 11:1; Zephaniah 3:17; Ephesians 1:11.

....

....

....

....

In your praise and worship, how much emphasis do you give to God as creator?

....

....

How much emphasis do these passages give to God's essential creativity? Genesis 1:1; Job 4:17; 35:10; 36:3; 38:1–39:30; Psalm 8:3; 95:6; 115:15; 119:73; 121:2; 124:8; 146:6; Isaiah 27:11; Jeremiah 10:16; Hosea 8:14; John 5:26; Romans 11:35–36; Hebrews 11:3; Revelation 3:14 & 4:11.

....

....

What does the Bible mean when it describes God as holy?

....

....

How does God's holiness effect his relationship with men and women?

....

....

What do all these verses teach about God? Genesis 18:14; Exodus 34:6–7; Deuteronomy 29:29; 1 Samuel 2:3; Nehemiah 9:17, 31; Psalm 59:10–17; 103:8; Jeremiah 32:27–28; Lamentations 3:22–23; Joel 2:13; Jonah 4:2; Zechariah 8:6; Hebrews 4:13; 1 John 4:8.

....

....

the name of god

The Bible records over three hundred different names of God, and these contain a rich revelation of his person, and of his purposes for humanity. Although each name reveals a distinct aspect of God's character, the phrase 'the name of God' or 'the name of the Lord' is itself frequently used in the Old Testament. This refers to the total revelation of all that is known about God. God is also often called 'the Name', especially in the New Testament.

With what do these verses from the Psalms associate God's name?

Psalm 33:21 ....

Psalm 89:15–16 ....

Psalm 89:24 ....

Psalm 96:2 ....

Psalm 99:3 ....

Psalm 100:4–5 ....

Psalm 109:21 ....

Psalm 138:2 ....

Psalm 138:2 ....

Psalm 148:13 ....

What do these verses teach about God's people and God's Name?

Psalm 5:11 ....

Psalm 52:9 ....

Psalm 54:6 ....

Malachi 4:2 ....

Psalm 99:6 ....

Isaiah 12:4 ....

Joel 2:26 ....

Micah 4:5 ....

Malachi 3:16 ....

GOD'S THREE 'ROOT' NAMES

1.   *Elohim*

In the Old Testament, God is identified over 2,500 times by the Hebrew word *Elohim*. In most English versions of the Bible, *Elohim* is simply translated as 'God'.

What does the name Elohim teach about God?

....

....

....

What is special about the Hebrew word Elohim?

....

....

Throughout the Old Testament, particular aspects of God's all-strong, all-mighty, all-majestic nature are revealed by adding Hebrew words to either *Elohim* or its shortened version *El*.

Re-read these verses, which each contain a name of God based in the Elohim root-name. After reading each verse, think of a situation or occasion when God has revealed this side of his character to you, and then pause to praise him using the name.

Joshua 24:19; Samuel 22:47; 2 Samuel 23:3; Psalm 43:2; Psalm 44:4; Isaiah 40:28; Isaiah 54:5; Psalm 84:9; Psalm 91:2; Jeremiah 10:10; Genesis 14:19; Genesis 16:13; Genesis 17:1; Exodus 20:5; Nehemiah 9:31; Nehemiah 9:32; Deuteronomy 7:9; Deuteronomy 32:4; Joshua 3:10; 1 Samuel 2:3; Psalm 68:19; Psalm 68:20; Psalm 77:14; Psalm 136:26; Isaiah 45:21.

2.   *Yahweh*

Yahweh is the common name of God, and is his first name, or his personal name. It is used over 6,800 times in the Old Testament. In older versions of the Bible, *Yahweh* is translated with capital letters as 'LORD' or 'GOD'. In most modern translations, it appears as 'Yahweh' to stress that this is God's personal name.

What does the name Yahweh teach about God?

....

....

Re-read these verses, which each contain a name of God based in the Yahweh root-name. After reading each verse, think of a situation or occasion when God has revealed this side of his character to you, and then pause to praise him using the name.

Genesis 22:14; Exodus 15:26; Exodus 17:15–16; Exodus 31:13; Judges 6:24; 1 Samuel 1:3; Psalm 23:1; Jeremiah 23:6; Ezekiel 48:35.

3. *Adonai*

Adonai is the least common of the three root names of God. It is used about 350 times in the Old Testament, and is always translated into English as 'Lord'.

What does the name Adonai teach about God?

....

....

FOUR *'TRUNK'* NAMES

Four divine names are used with great frequency; and we can think of them as '*trunk* names growing from the *root* names'. These reveal fundamental sides of God's nature and character.

1. *Yahweh Sabaoth*

God is called *Yahweh Sabaoth* about 200 times in the Bible, and this is usually translated in most English versions as 'the Lord of Hosts'.

What does the name Yahweh Sabaoth teach about God?

....

....

Describe a recent instance when God has revealed the Yahweh Sabaoth side of his character to you.

....

....

....

....

2.   *El Elyon*

El Elyon is generally translated as 'the Most High'. It is first used in Genesis 14:18, and is then used about another fifty times in the Old Testament.

What does the name El Elyon teach about God?

....

....

Describe a recent instance when God has revealed the El Elyon side of his character to you.

....

....

....

....

....

3.   *El Qodesh*

God is named as *El Qodesh* or *Qodesh* about sixty times in the Old Testament, and this is usually translated into English as 'the Holy One' or 'the Holy One of Israel'.

What does the name El Qodesh teach about God?

....

....

Describe a recent instance when God has revealed the El Qodesh side of his character to you.

....

....

....

....

....

....

This aspect of God's nature side of God is seen particularly clearly in God's revelation of himself in Exodus 34:6. We can think of this verse as God's 'amplified' name, and it is fundamental to the Jewish and Christian understanding of God.

Several forms of this name appear throughout the Old Testament – for example, 2 Chronicles 30:9; Psalm 86:15; 103:8; 116:5; Nehemiah 9:17, 31; Joel 2:13; Jonah 4:2 & Nahum 1:2.

How can we use this 'amplified name' in our personal and church lives?

....

....

....

....

4.   *El Shaddai*

In most older versions of the Bible, *El Shaddai* is translated as 'the Almighty', but this does not seem to fit with the way this name is used in the Old Testament. The Septuagint – the Greek version of the Old Testament – translated *El Shaddai* as 'the Sufficient', and this makes better sense as this name is almost always used in the context of God's extravagant provision.

What does the name El Shaddai teach about God?

....

....

Describe a recent instance when God has revealed the El Shaddai side of his character to you.

....

....

....

....

....

....

....

TWELVE *'BRANCH'* NAMES

There are twelve divine names which each appear about a dozen times. We can think of these as '*branch* names'. These names highlight important scriptural aspects of God's nature. We should recognise and remember the special emphasis that the Bible gives to them.

What are the twelve most common names?

Joshua 2:11 ....

Psalm 7:11 ....

Jeremiah 10:10 ....

1 Chronicles 28:9 ....

Jeremiah 10:16 ....

Psalm 18:2 ....

Nahum 1:2 ....

Judges 5:3 ....

2 Samuel 22:31 ....

Isaiah 43:3 ....

Habakkuk 3:19 ....

Daniel 6:20–26 ....

Which of these names are you most surprised to find on this list? Why are you surprised that this name is mentioned so often?

....

....

....

....

Which names are you surprised not to find on this list? Why do you think that they are not mentioned as often as you expected?

....

....

....

....

OTHER NAMES

There are about 200 names and titles of God which appear only once or twice in the Bible, and point to particular aspects of God's nature.

Re-read these verses, which each contain a name of God which appears only once or twice in the Bible. After reading each verse, think of a situation or occasion when God has revealed this side of his character to you, and then pause to praise him using the name.

Genesis 16:13; Genesis 21:33; Deuteronomy 6:4; Judges 6:24; 1 Samuel 2:3; 1 Chronicles 29:11; Psalm 4:1; Psalm 23:1; Psalm 42:8; Psalm 43:4; Psalm 62:5; Psalm 68:5; Psalm 77:1; Psalm 116:1; Proverbs 2:6; Song of Songs 1:3; Isaiah 41:4; Daniel 2:29; Daniel 7:9.

At the moment, which names of God do you use most frequently in your prayers and worship? Why do you use these particular names?

....

....

....

....

In this study, which name of God has made most impression on you? Why is this?

....

....

....

A series of beautiful descriptions of God are scattered throughout the Scriptures. While these are not actual names of God, there are wonderful descriptions of his nature in action.

Re-read these passages, which each contain an important description of God. After reading each passage, think how you could use it to praise God more creatively.

Exodus 15:11; 34:6–7; Leviticus 10:3; Numbers 6:24–27; Deuteronomy 4:35–39; 32:3–4; 32:39–41; 1 Samuel 2:6–10; 2 Samuel 22; 2 Kings 19:15–19; 1 Chronicles 16:8–36; 29:10–19; 2 Chronicles 14:10–11; 20:6; Nehemiah 9:5–38; Job 9:1–13; 11:7; 36:22–37:24; 38:1–39:30; Psalm 36:6–9; 86:15–16; 89:7–8; 91:1–2, 14–16; 103:1–6; 104:24–25, 34; 136; 145; 146:7–10; Jeremiah 32:17–20; Daniel 7:9–14; Habakkuk 3:1–19.

What is the most important truth that God has revealed to you about himself in this study?

....

....

....

....

the fatherhood of god

The New Testament shares the same basic understanding of God as the Old Testament, but focuses on fewer aspects of his nature.

In Matthew 8:11; 22:32; Luke 20:37; Acts 3:13 & 22:14, God is of called 'the God of Abraham, Isaac and Jacob'. And, in Revelation 1:8 & 21:6, God is called 'the Alpha and Omega'. What do these names teach us about God?

....
....
....
....
....

Which five aspects of God's nature are most stressed in the New Testament?

....
....
....
....
....

From the beginning of the New Testament to the end, the idea of God as Father is presented so frequently that his fatherhood has become a central feature of Christianity. In fact, God is not merely identified as 'Father' over 250 times in the New Testament, he is called 'Father' in every book except one.

THE FATHERHOOD OF GOD

It is Jesus who presents the fatherhood of God with most clarity. None of God's names was more constantly used by Jesus than 'Father'; and no other divine name seems to have so dominated his thoughts – both for his disciples and himself. Through Jesus, we learn that fatherhood is not one divine attribute among many, it is the central attitude which colours and shapes all the rest.

What do these passages teach about God's fatherhood?

Matthew 5:45; Luke 6:35; Acts 17:28–29.

....

....

Matthew 6:9, 32; Romans 8:15–17, 28; Galatians 4:6 & 1 Peter 1:17; Hebrews 12:5–7.

....

....

Matthew 11:27; Mark 1:11; 9:7; John 10:15–18, 29–30; 20:17; Romans 15:6; 2 Corinthians 11:31; Ephesians 1:3; 1 Peter 1:3.

....

....

OUR FATHER

What was especially radical about the 'Lord's Prayer' that Jesus taught his disciples?

....

....

How can we see the trunk names of God – El Elyon, Yahweh Sabaoth, El Qodesh and El Shaddai – in the Lord's Prayer?

....

....

....

....

....

....

In the light of the Old Testament, what does the phrase 'Our Father, Hallowed by your Name' teach about God?

....

....

....

It is vital we appreciate that 'our Father' is 'the Name'. Our intimate relationship with the Father must not diminish our awe in approaching him. We must not reduce the biblical view of God's fatherhood to the level of our human experience of fatherhood. Our earthly relationships with our parents will always be imperfect, but – in God – the perfect pattern of true parenthood is permanently seen.

What does Ephesians 3:14–15 teach about God's fatherhood?

....

....

What does Matthew 6:26–32 & 10:29–30 teach about God's fatherhood?

....

....

THE FATHER'S ATTRIBUTES

Just as God's nature in the Old Testament is revealed by adding words to his root names, so God's fatherhood in the New Testament is qualified to develop its richness.

What do these verses teach about God's fatherhood?

Matthew 5:16 ....

Matthew 5:48 ....

Matthew 6:1 ....

Matthew 6:4 ....

Matthew 6:8 ....

Matthew 6:14 ....

Matthew 6:26 ....

Matthew 7:21 ....

Matthew 11:25 ....

Matthew 26:53 ....

Matthew 28:19 ....

Luke 6:36 ....

John 3:35 ....

John 4:21–23 ....

John 5:17 ....

John 5:21 ....

John 5:26 ....

John 6:32 ....

John 8:28 ....

John 10:30 ....

John 17:11 ....

John 17:25 ....

2 Corinthians 1:3 ....

2 Corinthians 1:3 ....

Ephesians 1:17 ....

Hebrews 12:9 ....

James 1:17 ....

Romans 1:7 ....

Colossians 1:12 ....

Hebrews 12:5–11 ....

We need to remember that the New Testament does not define the Father's nature and attributes; instead, it contains a mass of incidents and examples which offer insights into his holy character and actions. It is not really possible to develop a systematic picture of divine fatherhood, but several main features of the Father's nature are clear:

1. His glory and power

The Father is supremely glorious, and Hebrews 1:3 shows that Jesus reflects his glory. This means that Christ presents the *whole* nature of God – his majesty, power, love *and* fatherhood.

In the last few months, what is your clearest experience of the Father's glory and power?

....

....

....

....

2.   His wisdom and will

Matthew 6:4–8; Ephesians 1:5 & 1 Peter 1:2 point to the Father's knowledge. As the Father is all-wise and all-knowing, his will, plans and purposes must be perfect.

In the last few months, what is your clearest experience of the Father's wisdom?

....

....

....

....

3.   His absolute holiness

We have seen that holiness is the most emphasised quality of God's name; and John 17:11 identifies God as 'holy Father'. The New Testament always makes it plain that the Father's character and actions are totally holy. He is completely set-apart; his purity is absolute.

In the last few months, what is your clearest experience of the Father's holiness?

....

....

....

....

4.   His righteousness and wrath

Jesus identifies God as 'righteous Father' in John 17:25, and the Father's righteousness is basic to the whole plan of salvation. The Father's wrath is an important aspect of his righteousness: it expresses the revulsion of his absolute holiness to all that is not holy.

In the last few months, what is your clearest experience of the Father's righteous wrath?

....

....

....

....

5.   His love and grace

1 John 3:1 sets God's love firmly in the context of his fatherhood. Love cannot exist in abstract; it must have an object. The New Testament clearly reveals that people are the objects of God's love, and that – within the Godhead – the Son is the object of the Father's love.

God's grace and mercy are closely linked with his love. The Father's grace means that he gives undeserved favours to the objects of his love, to his children.

In the last few months, what is your clearest experience of the Father's love and grace?

....

....

....

....

6.   His faithfulness and peace

1 Corinthians 1:9 sets God's faithfulness in the context of his fatherhood, and the wider New Testament teaching clearly shows that God is faithful: it constantly assumes that the unceasing and unchanging nature of God means the Father can be trusted to fulfil his promises.

All Paul's epistles begin with a blessing which includes 'peace from God'. There is no tension or worry within God. He is never uncertain about his actions or frustrated in his plans. His mind always maintains a perfect equilibrium. At the heart of the universe, behind all the chaos of human affairs, is the God of infinite peace.

In the last few months, what is your clearest experience of the Father's faithfulness?

....

....

....

....

Because God is eternal and infinite, no human understanding of him can ever be complete. No summary of biblical passages, no list of names and attributes, can ever present the *full* picture. The New Testament suggests, however, that we can know what we need to know about God.

What, for you, is the most important truth that you have learnt about the Father? What practical difference is this going to make to your life?

....

....

....

....

....

the father and the son

What 'hints' does the Old Testament contain about God's corporate nature?

....

....

....

....

....

....

The New Testament does not actually define God in terms of a Holy Trinity, it simply presents information which suggests that Jesus and the Spirit have a divine nature – and that they are one with each other and with God.

There are four groups of passages in the New Testament which, in different ways, imply that God's nature is essentially 'triune' or 'three-in-one'.

How do Matthew 28:19; 2 Corinthians 13:14; Revelation 1:4–8 point to a triune God?

....

....

....

How do Ephesians 1:3–14; 4:4–6; 1 Corinthians 12:3–6; 1 Peter 1:2 point to a triune God?

....

....

....

How do Mark 1:9–11; Luke 10:21; Romans 8; Galatians 4:4–6; 2 Thessalonians 2:13–14; Titus 3:4–6 and Jude 1:20–21 point to a triune God?

....

....

....

How do John 14:16–17, 25–26; 15:26; 16:13–15 point to a triune God?

....

....

....

As well as pointing to three distinct persons, the New Testament also emphasises the absolute unity or oneness of God. John 10:30 is the strongest statement, and Jesus' claim that 'the Father and I are one' prompted the Jews to fetch stones to kill him for blasphemy.

How do John 1:1; 8:24, 28; 10:30, 38; 14:9–11 & 17:21–23 point to the absolute oneness of the Father and the Son?

....

....

....

....

The New Testament stresses that God is one being whose essence exists eternally in three 'uni-persons'. It is vital we realise that the Father, the Son and the Spirit are three self-distinctions within one being, and not three distinct individuals. God is one, he is not divided into three, but he reveals his nature in a three-fold diversity of persons, characteristics and functions.

Many people – especially those in other religious groups – question the Christian understanding of a Holy Trinity. How would you explain the triune nature of God to an unbeliever?

....

....

....

....

....

....

....

....

THE FATHER AND THE SON

What do Matthew 11:25–30; Luke 10:21–22; Ephesians 5:19–20 teach about the role of the Spirit in knowing the Father?

....
....
....
....

How does the Son depend on the Father?

....
....
....

How does the Father depend on the Son?

....
....
....

Why is it important to know the Father/Son relationship of God?

....
....
....
....

THE FATHER'S IDENTITY

The New Testament teaches that it is God's nature and will for the Father to speak and act through his Son. This means that the Father expresses his identity in and through the Son.

John 1:18 reveals two important truths:

1. *the Father expresses his identity in the Son because it is the Son who has made him known*

2. *the Son is identical with the Father in being and nature*

Why must Jesus share the Father's divine nature and being to be an adequate and accurate revelation of the Father?

....

....

....

....

What does this truth mean for Jesus' ministry?

....

....

....

What does Jesus' life reveal about the Father?

....

....

....

THE FATHER'S PARTNERSHIP

The New Testament assumes that Jesus is the Father's essential partner in all God's dealings with humanity: the coming, living, dying, rising Jesus is the indispensable clue to the Father's purpose. While we cannot know the Father except by knowing the Son, we must not forget that we know the Son *so that* we can know the Father.

What do John 1:3; Colossians 1:15–17; Hebrews 1:2 teach about the Father's partnership with the Son?

....

....

....

What do John 3:16; 2 Corinthians 5:18–19 teach about this partnership?

....

....

....

*What do John 3:18; 5:22; Acts 17:31; Ephesians 1:10; Philippians 2:9–11; 1 Corinthians 15:28
teach about the partnership?*

....

....

....

....

What have you learnt about the Father through your study of the Father and the Son?

....

....

....

....

....

the father and the spirit

*What are some of the ways that the New Testament uses to reveal that the Holy Spirit is God,
yet is distinct from 'the Father' and 'the Son'?*

....

....

....

....

....

....

....

What two special declarations are the result of the Spirit's work in the lives of believers?

....

....

ABBA

The cry of praise, 'Abba Father', describes the way that we approach God as Father, in the access that the Spirit provides. The word 'Abba' makes it clear that the new name we use to address God is not one which we have chosen or invented. It comes from Jesus, who first spoke to God in this way.

Whenever we approach God praying 'Abba', we are acknowledging that we have learnt this way of approach from the Son. Our right to address God as 'Abba' comes from the Son, and is given to us by the Spirit – who takes what was first in Christ and makes it real for us. We approach the Father and call him 'Abba' through the Son and in the Spirit.

How did the first century Jewish understanding of fatherhood differ from ours today?

....

....

....

If the Father in the New Testament is more like a first century father than a modern-day father, what does this mean that he is like?

....

....

....

In the Old Testament, God is addressed as 'Father' only in the context of looking forward prophetically to Israel's final salvation.

What does Isaiah 63:7–16 teach about the relationship between the Father and the Spirit?

....

....

....

What do Psalm 89:19–26 and Isaiah 63:7–16 teach about the relationship between the Father, the Spirit and redemption?

....

....

....

What is the significance to you of Jesus addressing God as Abba in Gethsemane?

....

....

....

....

....

When the Spirit inspires us to cry 'Abba', what is he asking us to remember?

....

....

....

God has not always been the 'Abba' of everybody; instead, Jesus announces the gospel that God is his Father and that he wants to be our Father too – as we are drawn by the Spirit into the fellowship of faith and obedience which Jesus shows in Gethsemane. This means that the 'Our Father' is not a prayer for all people everywhere, it is the prayer of disciples who are following the one who cried 'Abba' in Gethsemane.

When do you pray the Lord's Prayer?

....

....

....

What does the Lord's Prayer mean to you?

....

....

....

How can we reclaim it as a special prayer for Gethsemane believers?

....

....

....

....

....

THE ACTIVITY OF THE SPIRIT

It is not enough to understand 'Abba', we also need to cry it in praise – and this is the work of the Spirit. God's fatherhood must be central not only to our *understanding* of God, but also to our *experience* of him. A Christian believer is not just a person who has been regenerated by the Spirit and converted to Christ, he is also a child who cries 'Abba' to the Father.

Is your Christian life more a relationship with Jesus, or a relationship with the Spirit, or a relationship with the Father?

....

Why is this?

....

....

....

How can you develop a deeper, more intimate, personal relationship with the Father?

....

....

....

How can we begin to cry 'Abba' to God, and start to know that we really are his children?

....

....

....

What does Romans 8:15–17 teach about being a child of the Father?

....

....

....

What should children reveal about the Father?

....

....

In the last few months, what have you revealed about the Father to your neighbours?

....
....
....
....
....

What is God's ultimate purpose for your life?

....
....
....
....

the father and the cross

What does Romans 1:18–32 teach about God's wrath and judgement?

....
....
....

Why does God act like this?

....
....

How can human rebellion and divine punishment be dealt with?

....
....
....

What do these passages teach about redemption? Mark 14:27; John 3:16; Romans 3:25; 4:25; 5:8; 8:3, 32; 2 Corinthians 5:18–21; 1 John 4:9–10.

....

....

What do you focus on when you think about the cross – in your praise, prayers, singing, etc?

....

....

Why is this?

....

....

The truth of the cross is that the Father gave the Son and the Son freely gave himself. The Father did not make the Son endure an ordeal that he was unwilling to bear, and the Son did not surprise the Father by his selfless action. This is set out in Galatians 1:4 & John 10:17–18.

This means we must recognise that the love and grace of the Father are not the result of redemption; they are its origin, its motivation, even its pre-condition. The obedience of the Son – in Gethsemane and on the cross – is merely a response to the love-filled will of the Father.

How, practically, can you help ensure that the Father's love in initiating redemption is better appreciated and celebrated?

....

....

....

....

What do these passages teach about redemption?

Romans 8:3 ....

....

2 Corinthians 5:18–19 ....

....

Philippians 2:6–8 ....

....

Hebrews 2:14–18 ....

....

1 John 4:10 ....

....

What are some reasons for believing that redemption must be the Father's action?

....

....

....

....

....

THE FATHER'S OUTCOME

Before the cross deals with human sin, it must deal with God's wrath. Therefore, on the cross, Jesus deals more with the Father than with us. On our behalf, he offers the obedient acceptance which fulfils the Father's will and bears the Father's judgement. He suffers the Father's abandonment, offers the trust which correspond exactly with the Father's, commends his work into the Father's hands, and awaits his verdict. The focus is all on the Father.

How does the Father respond to the Son?

....

....

....

This has considerable implications for our assurance. If our understanding of redemption focuses on our feelings about our forgiveness, our assurance will largely depend on the state of our personal emotions. If we do not feel forgiven, we will wonder whether we really are!

But our confidence in the cross does not depend on our feelings; it depends on the fact that the Father has said 'Yes' to the Son. This means that our assurance rests not in our subjective feelings about forgiveness, but in the objective fact of the resurrection – which is the Father's 'Yes' to the Son, to his work, and to all those on whose behalf the Son's work was undertaken.

The natures of the Father, the Son and the Spirit are identical, but their functions are distinct. The Father and the Son, for example, are equally and identically characterised by love and by sacrifice, but they are functionally distinct in that the Father wills and the Son executes the will, the Father sends and the Son is sent, the Father gives and the Son is given.

At the cross, what do the Father and the Son surrender and suffer?

The Son ....

....

The Father ....

....

What place should the Father's grief have in our understanding and celebration of the cross?

....

....

In what situations could somebody be helped by an appreciation of the Father's grief?

....

....

What does the story of the prodigal son teach about the Father?

....

....

....

What does the story of the prodigal son teach about the evangelistic message of forgiveness that we should proclaim?

....

....

....

....

What is the Father saying to you about your relationship with him?

....

....

....

....

the will of the father

For all sorts of historical, religious and philological reasons, any contemporary stress on obedience sounds hard and foreboding. But the 'gospel obedience', or 'living faith', that we see in Jesus is the exact opposite of 'legalistic obedience'. Satan delights to cause us to misunderstand important biblical words, and the common Christian understanding of obedience as 'legalistic' is one of his greatest successes.

In what basic ways does 'gospel obedience' differ from 'legalistic obedience?

1. ....

....

....

2. ....

....

....

3. ....

....

....

The general will and purpose for Jesus' life and ministry is set out in Luke 4:18–19; but Jesus did not live by a programme or principles, he lived from minute-to-minute by discerning what the will of God was in every situation.

As believers, we do not need divine guidance because we are ignorant of the Father's general will; we need guidance because we need insight into his particular will in different sets of circumstances. For example, we know that healing and wholeness are the Father's general-and-ultimate will for all people everywhere, but we need his particular will to know what to say and do when we are confronted by a sick person.

What does Acts 16:6–10 teach about the Father's general and particular will for Paul?

....

....

....

'ABBA' OBEDIENCE

Whenever we obey the Father's particular will, we join with Jesus in saying 'Abba' in Gethsemane. The words in Mark 14:36 are the archetype of all particular gospel obedience.

In Gethsemane, Jesus went to the Father to test his understanding of God's particular will that he must endure the cross on the morrow. Mark 8:31; 9:31 & 10:33–34 reveal that Jesus already knows God's general will, but he needs the Father's personal reassurance as to his particular will for that night and the following few days.

What has been your biggest struggle with God's particular will?

....

....

....

....

....

Jesus' purpose is not just to meet our needs. He always seeks to turn us into his disciples – into companions who want to follow him for his sake more than we want to use him to get things for our sake.

What can we learn from Luke 5:1–11 about moving from 'coming to God with a needs based approach' to 'going from God as a disciple'?

....

....

....

....

....

At the moment, what particular obedience is God calling you to?

....

....

....

....

....

THE PRIORITY OF THE FATHER'S WILL

How do you answer these questions? Please give some biblical reasons for your answers.

Is the Spirit's anointing free and unconditional? Or does he act in us only when we turn to him, and ask him and allow him to work?

. . . .

. . . .

. . . .

Do we have faith because the Spirit comes and creates that faith? Or does he come only when he finds faith already within us?

. . . .

. . . .

. . . .

Does the Spirit actively initiate faith in us? Or does he invite us, and then passively wait for us in our uninfluenced freedom to turn to him?

. . . .

. . . .

. . . .

Is the divine order 'grace then obedience', or 'obedience then grace'?

. . . .

. . . .

. . . .

What should the gospel message be if the order is 'obedience then grace'?

. . . .

. . . .

. . . .

What should the gospel message be if the order is 'grace then obedience'?

. . . .

. . . .

. . . .

One of the most burning questions for every believer to answer is how God's promises are fulfilled. We need to decide whether it is:

1. by our working through a list of conditions, and then performing a series of actions which match them;

2. by the Father in his grace leading us step-by-step towards the receiving of them – in his way and at his time.

Which do you believe to be the better answer? ....

Why is this? ....

....

....

What does this practically mean that you should do when God gives you a promise?

....

....

....

....

What do these passages teach about the human will and the Father's will?

Ephesians 1:4–6 ....

....

....

Ephesians 2:1–5 ....

....

....

Ephesians 2:8–9 ....

....

....

What is the most important truth that you have learnt in this section?

....

....

....

the father and prayer

In these passages, what are the different contexts within which God is called Father?

Matthew 5:16; 6:6; 11:25; 26:39, 53; Mark 14:3; Luke 10:21; 11:2; 23:34; John 11:41; 12:28; 14:16; 17:1, 5, 11, 26; Romans 8:15; 2 Corinthians 1:3; Ephesians 1:3; 2:18; 3:14; 5:20; Philippians 4:20; Colossians 1:3, 12; 3:17; James 3:9; 1 Peter 1:3, 17; Revelation 1:6.

....

....

....

....

What do these two passages teach about calling God 'Father'?

Galatians 4:6 ....

....

....

Ephesians 5:18–19 ....

....

....

At the moment, when you pray, do you generally address Jesus, or the Father, or the Spirit?

....

Why is this? ....

....

....

....

In the New Testament, it is plain that the Father should be the primary focus of prayer. Our prayer and praise may sometimes be directed to Jesus and to the Spirit; but the whole movement of the life of God has its source and its goal in the Father. As the Son and the Spirit are themselves from and for the Father, their chief aim in prayer is to introduce us to the Father and to establish us in fellowship with him.

It follows that most of our prayers should properly be addressed to the Father. We cannot pray apart from the Son and the Spirit, and they both teach us to pray, 'Abba Father'. Despite this, many believers address most of their prayers to Jesus – and teach their children to talk to Jesus.

Why do some believers focus more on Jesus in prayer than on the Father?

....

....

....

....

How, practically, does Jesus help you to pray?

....

....

....

....

How, practically, does the Spirit help you to pray?

....

....

....

....

How do you help others to pray?

....

....

....

....

How can we 'hallow God's name' today?

....

....

....

....

....

How has God most recently answered your prayer that his kingdom should come, and that his will should be done?

....

....

....

....

....

....

....

What can we learn from the order of the petitions in the Lord's Prayer?

....

....

....

....

....

....

....

....

What has God shown you about the Father and prayer?

....

....

....

....

What changes is God asking you to make to your prayer life?

....

....

....

....

....

'our' father

Matthew 5:45 and Luke 6:35 show that God's fatherly attributes are displayed even to 'the unthankful and the evil'. Jesus presents God as universal Father throughout the Sermon on the Mount, but he sets God's universal fatherhood in the context of God as Creator – this is particularly plain in Matthew 5:43–48 & 6:25–34.

The God who is the Father of his children is also the Creator of the whole world, and we can truly appreciate him as 'Our' Father only when we relate his fatherhood to his creatorship.

Which do you focus on more – God as Creator, God as Redeemer, or God as Father?

....

Why is this? ....

....

....

....

How can your church better communicate God's love as Creator for the whole world?

....

....

....

....

....

....

Why is it important to hold God's creatorship and fatherhood together?

....

....

....

....

When we say 'Our' Father, we are implicitly acknowledging that it is the Father's will and purpose for *all men and women* to live in grateful gospel obedience as his redeemed children.

THE WORLD OF THE FATHER

When we think about the work of the Son and the Spirit, it is easy to focus almost exclusively on matters like conversion, renewal and church life. But we need to appreciate that the Father, the Son and the Spirit are concerned with every aspect of creation, with the whole universe in all its physical and social realities.

John 3:16 declares that God so loved the whole world, the entire *kosmos*, that he gave his Son for it; and this suggests that we may need to think about salvation in bigger ways than we do.

How do you think about salvation at the moment?

....

....

....

What would it mean for you to have a bigger, 'whole-world' view of salvation?

....

....

....

What do these verses teach about God's ultimate purpose for all creation?

1 Corinthians 15:45 ....

....

....

2 Corinthians 4:6 ....

....

....

What do these verses teach about the church's role in attaining this ultimate purpose?

Romans 8:22–23 ....

....

....

Ephesians 3:10–11 ....

....

....

Which demonic 'powers and authorities' seem to influence your part of 'the world'?

....

....

....

....

How can your church reveal God's wisdom to these powers, and show them how they can be renewed and re-aligned by the Spirit into the different structures of the new creation?

....

....

....

....

....

....

Many Christians focus on the personal dimension of demonic beings, and concentrate on casting spirits from individual needy people. We should, however, be equally concerned with the sociological dimension of demonic powers, with our hurting world, and should seek God for gracious signs to disarm and overthrow these powers too.

Reread the suggestions on pages 118–119 as to how a local church can disarm these powers.

Which of these are most relevant to your church?

....

....

....

How, practically, can you begin to bring this about?

....

....

....

....

....

....

Which aspects of our Father's world are you most involved with?

....

....

....

What is holding you back from becoming more involved in the renewal of our Father's world and society?

....

....

....

....

How can you move on from 'My' Father to 'Our' Father, and become a prophetic sign to the Father's hurting world of the renewing, re-aligning power of the Son?

....

....

....

....

What is the most important truth that you have learnt about the Father in this book?

....

....

....

What changes is God asking you to make in your thinking and living?

....

....

....

What is the next step that God is asking you to take?

....

....

....